My Discovery of America

My Discovery of America

Vladimir Mayakovsky

Translated by Neil Cornwell

ET REMOTISSIMA PROPE

Modern Voices

Modern Voices
Published by Hesperus Press Limited
4 Rickett Street, London sw6 1RU
www.hesperuspress.com

My Discovery of America first published in Russian in 1926
This translation first published by Hesperus Press Limited, 2005

Introduction and English language translation © Neil Cornwell, 2005
Foreword © Colum McCann, 2005

Designed and typeset by Fraser Muggeridge studio
Printed in Jordan by Jordan National Press

ISBN: 1-84391-408-5

Contents

Foreword

The serious problems of life are never fully solved,
but some states can be resolved rhythmically.
                                    (Theodore Roethke)

And so there he is: standing above the East River in the grey of early evening, thirty-two years old, tall, booming, span-shouldered, a cigarette in his fingers, his metal-tipped boots against the wooden planks of the walkway, the hat carried at his waist, his suit jacket askew, looking along the harp-strung expanse of columns and cables, eager to get to the essence of it, the stretch of it, the jaunt of it, the breadth of it, the mystery: Brooklyn Bridge.

In the end it becomes his best American poem, perhaps as powerful as those written by Crane and Whitman. 'Brooklyn Bridge' – Mayakovsky's self-professed shout of joy – is a contemplation on the austere disposition of bolts and steel and how they can become, even in a society as undemocratic as New York's, a manifestation of the possibility of human vision. It is also a love poem and maybe, in its full-throated roar, a hint at what it means to be disillusioned by the political structures within the life of an individual.

See him there: turning between Brooklyn and Manhattan, between what was and what could be, between what is and what should have been. He is briefly happy – touching, he suggests, America's heart with his fingers – but really when he steps away, off the bridge, back into the city, where the garment workers he has met have few working rights, where the Negro poets he has befriended are drinking at different fountains to the whites, where the tenements he has passed are crumbling, where the choreography of commerce is the rich man's game, he must know in the end that the magnificent bridge is just another piece of human jewellery.

When we begin with Mayakovsky, we so often begin with his death. What a beautiful suicide note! What an awful mess the bullet made of his vocal chords!

Sometimes it seems that, in Europe and America in particular, we want to understand him through his death. It's often easier that way, especially for a complicated rattle-bag like Mayakovsky – a Futurist who practised empathy, a poet who praised technology, a dandy dresser who disdained riches, a loud expansive man who would often write only ten lines a day. He was interested in the living language of the street, its rhythm and noises. His article of faith – in the Soviet Union of all places – was that words functioned with the precision of machinery. He lived in the vanguard and rejected tradition. Pledged himself to the Revolution. He wrote poems that did not wait to be received – instead they went out and grabbed listeners by the scruff of the neck. In his younger years he would step onstage in outrageous costumes or interrupt the readings of other writers or scream drunkenly from the balconies. He sometimes bellowed his verse through a megaphone. In his older years he became progressively more satirical as he tried to reassemble his own innocence, restore himself to a radical state of consciousness, rekindle his belief in a politics that was his original flame.

In 1925 Mayakovsky, a seasoned traveller, went to Cuba, Mexico and the United States. He was announced by the New York Times as 'the generalissimo of the army of revolutionary minstrels'.

What we have in *My Discovery of America* is a series of reactions that he wrote primarily for Russian newspapers on his return to his native land. Some might deem it a pity that Mayakovsky didn't flex as full a muscle in his prose as he did in his poetry. (Brooklyn Bridge for instance doesn't get a look-in in the prose). Fair enough. It's true. He is not working here out of any overarching inner need except for whipping up his Soviet faithful. He is largely respectful of logic and grammar and so it ends up being little like experience: one is seldom allowed an intimate moment. His voice feels tired at times, hyperbolic at others, as if every night he's just brushing one tooth, indeed the same one constantly. He makes all sorts of geographical errors and outlandish simplicities. He also leaves out so many of the key events of his journey (for instance his friendship with David Burliuk, and his affair with Elly Jones, with whom, he was to discover, he had fathered a daughter).

It is a sorely unnatural thing when Mayakovsky tries to naturalise himself, if even just for a few months, in the Americas. He looks around and finds his distance announced everywhere.

And yet *My Discovery of America* is an unequivocally important document. Beyond the plain fact that it is an outsider's look at America in the pivotal 1920s (post-war, Prohibition, the throes of modernism, pre-Great Depression, etc.), it is also an intimate look at both the idealism and cynicism of the Communist eye.

Mayakovsky is enthralled by simple things and sometimes his voice soars. His great gift is his obvious empathy. He genuinely cares about the plight of the poor Cubans, the African-Americans of Harlem and the workers of Mexico. He has great fun poking a stick in the eye of cold capitalism. One can feel him stomping around noisily in his famous boots (always studded with metal) and reciting the wonderful Chicago section out loud.

In this series of sketches, Mayakovsky can also be interpreted as critiquing his own political system, processing (as he once wrote in a poem) the tons of verbal ore for the sake of a single word. He is, whether consciously or not, indicating that the truth when too tightly embraced can become a lie. There is a sense of darkness falling, not only over the Americas, but his own country too: the landscape of Russia and the contours of Mayakovsky's own imagination.

The labour of Mayakovsky's poetry was always to incite a decency of human spirit within a twentieth-century context, but he can be felt huffing and puffing with the sheer weight of what happens when you try to shine your own light in someone else's darkness. Lo and behold, it bounces back. ('No heavy boots please', he once wrote in his poem 'Cloud in Trousers', 'Tell the firemen to go gently when the heart's on fire'.)

And yet there is a sense of humour and irony in this work. Every now and then he deftly puts his finger on the pulse of the wound. Who could argue that his critique of America is not still relevant to this very day – 'there isn't a country that spits out as much moralistic, lofty, idealistic, sanctimonious rubbish as the United States', he writes – and maybe even more relevant given events of recent years.

He is seventy-five years dead now but Mayakovsky's echoes are still found today. They can, of course, be heard in the work of generations of Soviet writers (from the wonderful verses of Evgeny Evtushenko all the way through to Victor Pelevin), but there is also ample space to look at how Mayakovsky influenced the likes of Pablo Neruda, Nicanor Parra, Jack Kerouac, Allen Ginsberg and consequently many others in the Americas.

Mayakovsky's spoke of light was wide. It too, like his famous last note, still crashes against the shores of the everyday. In some ways he's still standing there on Brooklyn Bridge where he noted, in the grey light of evening, America's 'prolonged and hungry howl'.

– *Colum McCann, 2005*

Introduction

Vladimir Mayakovsky was (along with Velimir Khlebnikov) the leading Futurist poet in Russia over the last half-dozen years before the Revolution; subsequently he became Soviet Russia's outstanding poetic advocate – up until his sudden suicide, at the age of thirty-six, in April 1930.

As a Futurist, Mayakovsky had, as a matter of course, been fundamentally drawn to the new rather than the old – the future rather than the past. This disposition presupposed a commitment to the iconoclastic avant-garde in artistic forms, to scientific and technological advance, and to a new ideological and political system. Mayakovsky found all of these, and vigorously promoted them, over the first upbeat years of the post-October Bolshevik Soviet State. The artistic and especially the technological elements had long been associated with America – the land of dynamic development and untrammelled capitalism. In 1925, he was to observe for himself in America 'the futurism of naked technology'.

An early brief article by Mayakovsky, in which he claimed that life had now legitimised the antics of the Futurists, was entitled 'Now to the Americas' (1914). America, or the United States specifically, had featured in several of his poetic works – in particular the lengthy agitational epic of 1919–20, *150,000,000* (the figure denoting the population at that time of the U.S.S.R.). In this work of attempted myth creation, an ordinary Russian 'Ivan' is pitted against the head of world capitalism, Woodrow Wilson, who is located in that centre of advanced technology, Chicago (this poem being quoted later in *My Discovery of America*). Mayakovsky, along with others in the Soviet Union, envisaged miracles of production in the Communist future, but saw the United States (albeit the main ideological opponent) as the obvious and necessary technological model for Soviet development.

Mayakovsky, in the 1920s, became an indefatigable traveller. The reasons for this ranged from pure curiosity and a desire for renewed artistic inspiration to personal restlessness, boredom and frustration with the complex manoeuvrings of Soviet cultural politics, and amorous crises. These last were liable to arise out of difficulties in the apparently civilised *ménage à trois* shared with his long-standing mistress Lili and her husband, the critic and editor Osip Brik, or later from complications in a new love relationship. One such crisis with Lili Brik was immortalised in the remarkable narrative poem *About This* (or *About That*), published in 1923 in *LEF* (with its memorable cover image of Lili), the journal of the artistic movement Mayakovsky had founded together with his friend Osip. In any event, Mayakovsky visited Riga, Berlin and Paris in 1922, and again in 1924; just Berlin was visited in 1923. He made journeys to two or three dozen Soviet towns in 1926 and 1927, as well as Prague, Berlin, Paris and Warsaw; his last trips to Paris in 1928 and 1929 led to a final and apparently disastrous love affair. However, in the summer of 1925 he undertook his famed voyage to the Americas – as the start of what might have been (but in the event was not) a round-the-world trip.

Making his way overland to an Atlantic port, Mayakovsky got off to a poor start when all his money was stolen in Paris – by a 'highly talented thief'. This resulted in severe financial constraints and necessitated constant borrowing. It probably caused him to abort his trip round the world and it required him to travel third class on the return voyage, having managed a first-class ticket outward bound – the contrast being well marked up in his travelogue. He made little or no money from his lectures and readings, organised by left-wing Russian and Jewish elements in the United States and backed by the American Communist and immigrant press (*New Masses*, the *Daily Worker*, *Russian Voice* and others).

Mayakovsky had considerable difficulty, for obvious political reasons, in obtaining a visa to enter the United States. The problem was ironed out by his old friend, the Futurist painter and poet David Burliuk, who had been resident in the States since the early 1920s. Not mentioned in *My Discovery of America*, Burliuk does make an appearance in *How I Made Her Laugh*, the short companion piece printed in the present volume (which relates to Mayakovsky's Soviet homecoming). Mayakovsky was initially to be admitted to the United States as a 'commercial artist' (which indeed, among other things, he was – as the author of state-backed illustrated advertising jingles). The visa situation made a circuitous route to New York advisable. Mayakovsky therefore took a boat bound for Mexico (Vera Cruz), with a stop in Havana. The Mexican episode proved a rewarding one for Mayakovsky, and resulted in some of the most colourful pages in his memoir. He finally entered the United States at the border crossing point of Laredo, Texas, on 27th July 1925 – arriving in New York by train on 30th July.

From New York, the 'plenipotentiary of Soviet poetry', as Mayakovsky liked to style himself, visited Rockaway Beach, Cleveland, Detroit, Chicago, Philadelphia and Pittsburgh. Foolishly, one may well think, he turned down an invitation to lecture in San Francisco and hurried back to New York, where he caught a French steamer back to Europe on 28th October. He had used up just three months of his six-month permit. Financial considerations apart, he cited, as his reasons for this, boredom and solitude, nostalgia for the homeland, and, in particular, his absence from Lili.

Mayakovsky seems not to have sent letters from America. He did however send a number of telegrams to Lili Brik, protesting loneliness, boredom and his love. There have been personal reminiscences relating to his American visit, and newspaper reports of his activities. One account speaks of a rather wild party, organised by the Communist journal *New Masses*, with vigorous dancing and (presumably illegal) gin-swilling, during which Mayakovsky admitted: 'Yes, I am a bohemian. That is my great problem: to burn out all my bohemian past, to rise to the heights of the Revolution.' There were, however, some stages of his American sojourn unaccounted for. Mayakovsky's 'bohemianism' stretched in fact to a two-month love affair, from which an American daughter was the result. Although rumours and coy references had been rife for two thirds of a century, the seriousness of this relationship, and the identities of mother and daughter, remained almost a total secret until the early 1990s. In 1993, marking the Mayakovsky centennial, the daughter herself (who even remembers her father from meeting him in Nice, at the age of two!) brought out a book. Patricia J. Thompson's [aka Yelena Mayakovskaya] volume *Mayakovsky in Manhattan: A Love Story, with Excerpts from the Memoir of Elly Jones* [her mother] was published in a limited edition (by West End Productions, New York).

The main records of Mayakovsky's American visit, though, are the artistic ones: these comprise the poetic cycle of *Poems about America*, subsequently published as a separate collection; and the journalistic travelogue – sketches that appeared in various Soviet outlets and were later collected and edited to form *My Discovery of America*. A number of the poems have their descriptive counterpart within the prose text. These, of course, feed very much, if not exclusively, into what the Formalist critic Boris Tomashevsky saw as the biographical legend created by the author himself. 'Only such a legend is a *literary fact*,' Tomashevsky declared; and the life of Mayakovsky is rich, above all, in such literary facts.

The *Poems about America* were written mostly in America, and recited to audiences there, with the 'framing' poems penned on the outward voyage ('The Atlantic Ocean'), and the return one ('Homeward!'), and some a little later. 'The Atlantic Ocean' is a meditation on the qualities of the ocean and revolution. Like much of Mayakovsky's poetry of the 1920s, the twenty-two American poems are wide in range and uneven in quality, expressing the tensions (both arising within Mayakovsky's muse and reflected in perceptions thereof) between the often irrepressible agitational urge and the powerful lyrical gift. The poem 'Mexico' may be seen as a successful combination of these elements. 'Broadway' is an innovative exercise in urban imagery and verbal play. However, 'Brooklyn Bridge', in which the remains of New York are examined by a 'geologist' of the future, is considered Mayakovsky's supreme American poetic achievement.

The prose travel notes, here presented in full for the first time in English translation, were written hurriedly and published piecemeal – in part to assist the recovery of their author's badly hit finances. Regarded in some quarters as 'hack work' (*khaltura*), *My Discovery of America* would never have been recommended as a reliable travel guide to North America – nor, of course, was it ever intended to be. Mayakovsky was quite capable of confusing New York railway stations; of failing to distinguish between the Hudson and the East Rivers; and of re-construing a Vanderbilt Hotel (on Fifth Avenue, sold during his stay) as Miss Vanderbilt's 'palace' (supposedly disposed of by her due to the proximity of despised small businesses). For that matter, his command of English (as of other foreign languages) ranged from the all but non-existent to the minimal, allowing him seemingly to transpose the then widely used appellation of 'Mac' into the alleged American 'greeting' of 'Make money?' (*Mek monei*). Mayakovsky is strongly interested in political matters and union affairs; his reportage of America stems natur-ally from his own political outlook and depends largely on the limited sources on which he relied: the American (or mainly

Russian immigrant) Communist press and his Russian-American friends and contacts.

Nevertheless, Mayakovsky does provide an idiosyncratic and impressionistic, and perhaps indeed a unique, depiction of mid-1920s pre-Depression America, and (in the first third of the narrative) Mexico. Apart from aspects of his own psychological make-up, Mayakovsky puts into *My Discovery of America* something of the constructivist approach to 'production art', the *LEF*-inspired precepts of 'literature of fact' (*literatura fakta*) and the 'social commission' (*sotsial'nyi zakaz*). These are qualities not always seen in a very positive light, especially as they developed, post-1932, into 'socialist realism'. Here they are made much more palatable by Mayakovsky's more personal and wide-eyed reactions to what he observed, often expressed through the 'Formalist' device of 'making strange' (*ostranenie*) – now more widely known as 'defamiliarisation'. As earlier commentators have put it, Mayakovsky displayed a 'predilection for hyperbole and for presenting the mundane in an out-of-the-ordinary light' – and not just the mundane, one might add.

Written, of course (certainly primarily), for a Soviet Russian readership, *My Discovery of America* observes, and in the main celebrates, modernisation, industrialisation and especially electrification (Lenin – no lover of most of Mayakovsky's work – might have been proud of him here!). And this Soviet cultural agent is here advocating for the U.S.S.R. a limited form of Americanisation. Mayakovsky has a vision: that the right assimilation of this 'primitive futurism' can mean 'a second discovery of America – for the benefit of the U.S.S.R.'. Much of Mayakovsky's work was produced 'at the top of his voice' and the American travelogue too, which includes a number of 'tales' or anecdotes, often adopts a declamatory style (*How I Made Her Laugh*, indeed, reads almost as a stand-up monologue). For all its propagandistic slant and political point-scoring (which is not, however, without an infusion of acute social comment), much of this memoir of the Americas is delivered in an ironic tone and with characteristic Mayakovskian humour. This quality is particularly evident, perhaps, in the scenes in Havana and Mexico (especially the bullfight passage), in the self-deprecating cameo at Coney Island, and in the remarks on American trains. What really sticks in the mind, though, are the double-edged perorations on technology and the fascination with the phenomenon, and the spectacle, of illumination.

For the twenty-first-century reader, interest may be largely in the depiction, by an eloquent outsider, of America (or indeed, as Mayakovsky would prefer it, the Americas) at a particular point of historical and social development. What, even now, appears much the same, and what – the best part of a century later – has changed? Which of Mayakovsky's hopes, fears or predictions have, to any real degree at all, been borne out? Mayakovsky's American daughter, writing in 1993, emphasises that 'Mayakovsky wrote his observations of the United States with brutal honesty – an honesty that rings true even today'.

My Discovery of America also preserves an inspirational, and for him exotic, interlude in Mayakovsky's private, public and artistic development, before an encroaching tide of solitude – personal, aesthetic, intellectual, existential and political – led him to fulfil the prophecy foretold by the title of his first play, *Vladimir Mayakovsky: A Tragedy*.

– *Neil Cornwell, 2005*

Note on the Text:

The texts translated here are taken from Vol. VII of Vladimir Mayakovsky, *Polnoe sobranie sochinenii* [*Complete Collected Works*], in thirteen volumes, published by Gos. izd. Khudozhestvennoi literatury, Moscow, 1958. In addition to this edition, I have consulted the large extract (pertaining to Mayakovsky's U.S.A. travels) translated by Olga Peters Hasty and Susanne Fusso, and included in the anthology *America Through Russian Eyes, 1874-1926* (Yale University Press, 1988). I am also indebted to Edward J. Brown's monograph, *Mayakovsky: A Poet in the Revolution* (Princeton University Press, 1973), which remains the best all-round study of Mayakovsky.

The present translation is intended, in part at least, as a testimonial to the Mayakovsky and Pasternak 'Special Subject' course of 1971–72 at the School of Slavonic and East European Studies, University of London. This class was attended by Liz Barnes, Pete Saunders and Vera Vargassoff, together with the present translator – and taught with great expertise and enthusiasm by the late Nick Anning.

My Discovery of America

Mexico

TWO WORDS. My latest route – Moscow, Königsberg (by air), Berlin, Paris, Saint-Nazaire, Gijón, Santander, Cape La Coruña (Spain), Havana (the island of Cuba), Vera Cruz, Mexico City, Laredo (Mexico), New York, Chicago, Philadelphia, Detroit, Pittsburgh, Cleveland (the North-American United Sates), Le Havre, Paris, Berlin, Riga, Moscow.

I absolutely have to travel. Contact with living things is almost replacing for me the reading of books.

Travel is satisfying enough for the reader of today. Instead of invented fancies about boring old things and figures and metaphors, you get real things, of interest in themselves.

I have lived too little to be able to describe every detail accurately and thoroughly.

This little I have lived is enough, though, to be able to render the miscellaneous faithfully.

EIGHTEEN DAYS ON THE OCEAN. The ocean – it's a matter of imagination. On the ocean you're out of sight of land, on the ocean there are more waves then there is any need for in everyday life, and on the ocean you have no notion of what is beneath you.

It's only imagination that to the right there's no land as far as the pole and that to the left there's no land as far as the pole, ahead there's an altogether new, secondary light, and under you, perhaps, is Atlantis – this is just the imaginative power of the Atlantic Ocean. A calm ocean is tedious. We are crawling for eighteen days, like a fly over a mirror. There was a well-staged spectacle just once, on the return voyage from New York to Le Havre. A continuous downpour lathered the white ocean, streaked the sky with white, and sewed sky and water together with white threads. Then there was a rainbow. The rainbow was reflected, locked in the water, and we were like circus performers, falling into the iridescent hoop. Then once again it is the floating sponges, the flying fish, the flying fish and again the floating sponges of the Sargasso Sea and, on rare gala occasions, the gushing of whales. And the whole time there is the wearisome (to the point of nausea) water and yet more water.

You get really fed up with the ocean, but it's boring without it.

Then it needs such a long time for the water to get roaring, for the engines to strike up soothingly, for the brass fittings on the hatches to rattle away rhythmically.

THE STEAMSHIP 'ESPAGNE', 14,000 tonnes. It's a small ship, rather like our 'GUM'.[1] Three classes, two funnels, one cinema, a cafeteria dining room, a library, a concert hall and a newspaper.

A newspaper called *The Atlantic*. However, it's not much of a thing. On the front page are the great figures Baliev and Shaliapin,[2] inside there's a write-up of some hotels (material that was obviously stocked up ashore), and a meagre column of latest news, today's menu and the latest from the radio – of the 'all quiet in Morocco' type.

The deck is decorated with coloured lanterns and in first class they dance all night with the officers. All night jazz is bashed out:

Marquita,
Marquita,
Marquita my love!
Oh why,
Oh Marquita,
Can't you love me true...

The classes fall out quite naturally. In first class you get merchants, manufacturers of hats and collars, artistic big shots and nuns. Strange people: Turkish by nationality, speaking only in English, living always in Mexico – representatives of French firms with Paraguayan and Argentinian passports. These are today's colonists, Mexican type. Just as earlier in return for shoddy trinkets the companions and the descendants of Columbus cleaned out the Indians, so now, for a red tie as the black man's introduction to European civilisation, they break the redskins' backs on the plantations of Havana. They keep to themselves. They only go into the third or the second class after pretty girls. In second class you get small-time travelling salesmen and apprentice intellectuals, who bang away at their Remingtons. Unnoticed always by the crew, they worm their way on to the first class decks. They strike an attitude, as if to say, I'm no different from you: I'm wearing collars and cuffs too. But they *are* different, and they're asked, almost politely, to go back where they belong. Third class – is mere hold freight: economic migrants from the Odessas of the whole world – boxers, snoops, Negroes.

They steer clear of the upper decks. They ask those dropping in from the superior classes, in a tone of sullen envy: 'Been playing whist?' From down there wafts up a stuffy odour of sweat and footwear, a rancid stink of drying nappies, the creaking of hammocks and campbeds thronging the whole deck, the ear-splitting howls of children, and the almost Russian whispering of the mothers trying to calm them: 'Hush now, moy sobbing pet.'[3]

In first class they play poker and mah-jong. In second it's chess and the guitar. In third – one person puts an arm behind their back, closes their eyes, and from behind someone smacks the palm of their hand as hard as they can, and you have to guess who out of the whole gang has hit you. And then the one recognised replaces the one who was hit. I recommend our students to try this Spanish game.

The first class puke up wherever they like; the second – down over the third class; and the third – over themselves.

Nothing happens.

A telegraphist comes along, yelling something about on-coming ships. It's possible to send a radio message to Europe.

The head of the library, in view of the lack of demand for books, is busy with other things too. He takes round slips with ten numbers. You pay ten francs and write down your name: if the number of miles covered turns up on yours, you get a hundred francs from this nautical tote.

My linguistic lack and my silence were construed as a diplomatic silence and one of the merchants, whenever meeting me, to maintain acquaintance with a top-class passenger, for some reason would yell out 'Pleven, good!' – two words he had learnt from a Jewish girl from deck three.

On the day before our arrival in Havana the ship came to life. A tombola was held – a nautical charitable event in aid of maritime orphans.

In first class they put on a lottery, drank champagne and genuflected at the name of a businessman called Maxton, who had donated two thousand francs. This name was posted on the announcement board, and Maxton's chest, amid general applause, was adorned with a tricoloured ribbon stamped in gold with his – Maxton's – surname.

The third class also held their festivities. But any loose change that the first and second classes throw into the hat, they collect for their own gain.

The highlight was the boxing. Obviously, this was for the fans of this sport, the English and the Americans. None of them knew how to box. It's repulsive – belting each other in the mug in the heat. In the first pairing was the ship's cook – a disrobed, puny, hairy Frenchman with black socks full of holes over his bare legs.

The cook was battered for some while. For about five minutes he held his own through skill and for another twenty minutes through pride, but then gave in, lowered his hands and went off, spitting out blood and teeth.

In the second bout, some fool of a Bulgarian, who arrogantly left his chest wide open, was scrapping with an American detective. This detective, a boxer of professional standard, was seized with fits of laughter. He flailed around but, through hilarity and surprise, was wide of the mark and broke his own hand, which had mended badly after a war-wound.

In the evening, the referee went round trying to collect money for the injured cop. We were all told in confidence that this detective was supposed to be on a top-secret assignment in Mexico and would now have to rest up in Havana, but no one will help out the one-armed cop – why should anyone help the American police?

This I could quite understand, seeing that even the 'American' referee in the straw helmet turned out to be a Jewish cobbler from Odessa.

And an Odessan Jew needs to be in on everything – even intervention on behalf of a secret agent he doesn't know under the tropic of Capricorn.

The heat is terrible.

A drink of water is useless: it immediately evaporates in sweat.

Hundreds of ventilators turned on their axles and rhythmically swung and twisted their heads – fanning the first class.

Now the third class hated the first class all the more, for being a degree cooler.

In the morning, scorched, baked and boiled, we approached the white – with both its buildings and its cliffs – port of Havana. A customs launch stuck itself on to us, and then came dozens of little boats, and even scruffier boats, laden with the spuds of Havana – pineapples. The third class threw down some coins and then pulled up a pineapple by a string.

On two competing boats, two residents of Havana were swearing at each other in pure Russian: 'Where d'you think you're going with your pines, you motherf…'

HAVANA. We were stuck there for days. Taking on coal. In Vera Cruz there's no coal, and it's needed for six days of voyage, there and back across the Gulf of Mexico. They immediately gave the first class a shore pass, delivered to everyone in their cabin. Merchants in their white silks scampered off excitedly with dozens of suitcases – samples of braces, collars, gramophones, hair-cream and red ties for Negroes. The merchants came back drunk in the night, boasting of the two-dollar cigars they had been given.

The second class disembarked selectively. Those the captain liked were let ashore – usually women.

The third class were not allowed off at all. They just hung around on deck amid the scraping and the crashing of the coal suction, amid the black dust sticking to the sticky sweat, tugging up their pineapples on a string.

Just when we were getting off it poured with rain – a tropical cascade which I had never seen before.

What is rain?

It's air with a film of water.

Tropical rain – that's sheer water with a film of air.

I'm a passenger from first class. I'm ashore. I shelter from the rain in a monstrous two-storey warehouse. The warehouse is crammed full from floor to ceiling with whiskey. Mysterious inscriptions – 'King George', 'Black and White', 'White Horse' – are written in black on the boxes of spirits – contraband, pouring out of here to the nearby dry United States.[4]

Behind the warehouse is the seaport filth of taverns, brothels and rotten fruit.

8

Behind the seaport strip lies a clean, very rich and cosmopolitan city.

One side is super-exotic. Against a sea-green background a black man in white trousers is selling a crimson fish, holding it by the tail high above his head. The other side – you find world-famous tobacco and sugar limited companies, with their tens of thousands of black, Spanish and Russian workers.

And in the centre of these riches there is the American club, the ten-storey Ford building, Clay and Bock[5] – the first tangible signs of the sway held by the United States over all three Americas: North, South and Central.

They own almost all of Havana's answer to Kuznetsky Most: the long, straight Prado, with its cafés, its advertising and its street lights. All around the Vedado,[6] in front of their residences entwined in pink *colario*,[7] are flamingos the colour of daybreak, standing on one leg. Indispensable police officers, on their low stools under parasols, watch over the Americans.

Everything to do with traditional exoticism is colourfully poetic and non-profitable. An example is the very beautiful cemetery of the multitudinous Gomez and Lopez breeds, with its dark alleys, even in daytime, of some sort of interwoven tropical and bewhiskered trees.

Everything to do with the Americans is adapted in an assiduous and well-organised fashion. At night I stood for about an hour in front of the windows of the Havana telegraph office. People were wilting in the Havana heat and writing almost inanimately. Under the ceiling along an endless tape fly receipts, forms and telegrams gripped in iron talons. The clever machine politely accepts a telegram from a young lady, passes it to the telegraphist and comes back from him bringing the latest world exchange rates. And in complete union with this, from the same power source, the ventilators revolve and swing their heads round.

It was all I could do to find the way back. I remembered the street by the enamel plate with the inscription '*tráfico*' – as though this was clearly the name of the street. Only a month later did I realise that the sign '*tráfico*' on thousands of streets simply indicates vehicular direction. Just before the ship's departure I rushed off for some magazines. On the square I was accosted by a ragamuffin. I could not immediately make out that he was asking for help. The ragamuffin expressed surprise:

'Do yu spik eenglish? Parlata espaniola? Parlay voo fransay?'

I kept quiet and in the end muttered brokenly, to shake him off: 'Aye em Ressia!'

This was the most precipitate of actions. The ragamuffin grabbed my hand with his two hands and roared:

'Hip Bolshevik! Aye em Bolshevik! Hip, hip!'

I stole away under the perplexed and wary glances of the passers-by.

We were already sailing out to the Mexican National Anthem.

How people are enriched by a National Anthem! Even the merchants turned serious, jumping up exhilaratedly from their chairs to bawl out something like:

> *Be prepared, oh Mexican*
> *to gallop off on your horse…*

At dinner they served food that was quite unfamiliar to me – a green coconut with the core dripping in oil and mango fruit, a caricature of a banana with a large hairy stone.

That night I looked jealously at the dotted line of lights far away to the right-hand side. This was the glitter of the Florida railway line.

On the iron posts in third class, the ones to which the ropes are tied, I was sitting – there were just the two of us – with a typist from Odessa who was emigrating. The typist was telling me tearfully:

'We lost our jobs. I was starving and my sister was starving, and this cousin once removed of ours from America told us to come over. So we got away and for a year now we've been sailing and travelling from country to country, and from town to town. My sister has quinsy and an abscess. I called the doctor. He didn't come, but told us to go to him. We went in and he says – get undressed. He sits there with someone else and just laughs. In Havana we wanted to get off like stowaways, but they pushed us back on. Pushed us right in the chest. It hurt. Just like in Constantinople, and in Alexandria. We're third class all right... This never happened in Odessa. Then there'll be two years to wait before they'll let us into the United States from Mexico... You're lucky! You'll be seeing Russia again in six months.'

MEXICO. Vera Cruz. A miserable-looking shoreline with small stunted houses. A round pavilion for the musicians who greet the boat with their bugles.

A platoon of trainee soldiers is marching on the shore. The ship has been tied up. Hundreds of little men in hats half a metre wide were shouting and stretching out their arms banded with porters' numbers[8] as far as the second deck, fighting with each other over suitcases, and then making off, collapsing under huge loads. Then they would return, wipe their faces, and start yelling and pestering once more.

'But where are the Indians?' I asked my neighbour.

'These are the Indians,' my neighbour replied.

I was mad about Indians, out of Cooper and Mayne Reid,[9] until the age of twelve. And here I stand, dumbstruck, as though before my very eyes peacocks were being turned into chickens.

I was well rewarded for my initial disappointment. Immediately beyond the customs house there began an incomprehensible, idiosyncratic and amazing way of life.

The first thing was a red flag with a hammer and sickle in the window of a two-storey building.

And this flag had nothing whatever to do with any Soviet consulate. It was the 'Prow Organisation'. A Mexican moves into an apartment and hoists a flag.

This means: 'I'm pleased to have moved in, and I won't be paying any rent.' And that's it.

Just try – and you'll be chucked out.

Brown-skinned people walk in the narrow shade of the walls and fences. It is possible to walk in the sun too, but only very slowly – otherwise you'll get sunstroke.

I was late realising this and for two weeks I walked around blowing out through my nostrils and my mouth, so as to make up for the insufficiency of rarefied air.

All life – business, meeting people, eating – it all goes on under the striped canvas awnings on the streets.

The main people are the shoeshine boys and the lottery ticket sellers. What the shoeshine boys live on, I don't know. The Indians go barefoot, and even if they do have anything on their feet, then it's something that would beggar both cleaning and description. And for everyone who does have shoes, there are at least five shoeshine boys.

But there are even more lottery sellers. They are about in their thousands, with their millions of winning tickets printed on cigarette paper cut into the smallest possible slips. And the next morning there are all the winnings with loads of piddling payouts. This is no real lottery, but some sort of a peculiar, alternative card game of chance. But the tickets get bought up like sunflower seeds in Moscow.

People don't hang around in Vera Cruz for long: they buy a

knapsack, change some dollars, sling their knapsack with their silver coins over their shoulders, and off they go to the station, to buy a ticket to the Mexican capital – Mexico City.

In Mexico they all carry their money around in bags. The frequent changes of government (over a stretch of twenty-eight years there were thirty presidents) undermined trust in all forms of paper money. Hence the bags.

And in Mexico there's banditry. I must confess that I can quite understand the bandits. And you, if bags of gold were jangling in front of your noses, wouldn't you have a go at it?

At the station I saw my first military types close up. A large hat with a feather, yellow face, moustaches two feet long, broadsword down to the floor, green uniforms and lacquered yellow leggings.

The Mexican army is fascinating. No one, the armed forces minister included, knows how many soldiers there are in Mexico. Soldiers are under generals. If a general is for the president, he, with a thousand soldiers, claims to have ten thousand. And, receiving supplies for ten thousand, he sells off the food and equipment for the other nine.

If a general is against the president, he parades a figure of a thousand, and then at the vital moment fields a fighting force of ten thousand.

For this reason the armed forces minister replies to questions on the quantity of troops:

'*Quién sabe, quién sabe*. Who knows, who knows? Maybe thirty thousand, but there could be even a hundred thousand.'

The troops live in the old way – under canvas with their bits and pieces, their wives and their children.

The bits and pieces, wives and children of such a rabble – they all take to the field at any time of civil strife. If one army is out of cartridges but has maize, but the others are without maize but have cartridges, then the armies break off their engagement while the families proceed to barter. One lot will stuff themselves with maize while the others fill their pouches with cartridges – and then they'll get on with the battle again.

On the way to the station, our motor car frightened a flock of birds. And that was really something to be frightened of.

The size of geese and as black as crows, with bare necks and huge beaks – they soared up in front of us.

These are *zopilotes*,[10] the peaceable crows of Mexico; their concern is with any kind of garbage.

We set off at nine in the evening.

The rail route from Vera Cruz to Mexico City is, they say, the most beautiful one in the world. At a height of nine thousand feet it rises along precipices, between cliffs and through tropical forests. I don't know. I didn't see it. But the tropical night which passed by the carriage was quite something.

In a completely blue, ultramarine night, the black silhouettes of the palms looked absolutely like long-haired bohemian artists.

The sky and the land merge. Both on high and low down there are stars. Two arrays. Above – are the motionless, accessible heavenly bodies; and below – the darting and flitting sparkle of fireflies.

When stations are lit up, you can see piles of filth, donkeys and long-hatted Mexicans wearing a *serape* – a striped rug, with a hole cut in the middle, so the head can be stuck through and the ends hang down over the front and the back.

They will stand and stare – but movement is no business of theirs.

Hanging over all this is a nauseating compound smell – a strange mixture of the stink of gasoline with a whiff of rotting banana and pineapple.

I was up early and went out onto the platform of the carriage.

Everything seemed the wrong way round.

I had never seen such a land, and didn't think there were such lands.

Against the background of a red sunrise stood cacti, themselves all stained with red. Just cacti. The nopals – favourite delicacy of donkeys – stand there listening, like enormous ears covered in warts. Like long kitchen knives, originating from the one spot, grows the maguey. This is distilled into a half-beer, half-vodka, called *pulque*, to addle the brains of the hungry Indians. And after the nopal and the maguey, at five times human height, there is also something that looks like pipes growing together, like a conservatoire organ, only dark green, with needles and cones.

That's the sort of route by which I approached Mexico City.

DIEGO RIVERA met me at the station.[11] And therefore painting was the first thing I got to know about in Mexico City.

I had earlier only heard that Diego was one of the founders of the Mexican Communist party, that Diego is the greatest Mexican artist, and that Diego can hit a coin in flight from a Colt. And I also knew that Erenburg had tried to write his *Julio Jurenito* with Diego.[12]

Diego turned out to be a huge man with a good stomach on him, and a broad face that was always smiling.

He talks about thousands of interesting things, mixing in Russian words (Diego understands Russian extremely well), but he warns me first:

'Bear in mind that even my wife will confirm that half of everything I tell you is exaggeration.'

From the station, having dumped my things in a hotel, we made off to the Mexican Museum. Diego moved in a throng, responding to hundreds of greetings, shaking the hands of those nearest and exchanging shouts with those walking down the other side of the street. We looked at ancient round Aztec calendars on stone from the Mexican pyramids, and double-snouted wind idols, whose faces caught up with each other.

We looked, and it was not for nothing that I was being shown all this. Already the Mexican consul in Paris, Mr Reyes, a well-known Mexican novelist, had warned me that, according to today's ideas, Mexican art is an outgrowth from the ancient, variegated, primitive, folkloric Indian art, and not from the imitative eclectic forms brought over from Europe. This idea is a part – though perhaps not yet a realised part – of the idea of struggle and liberation from colonial slavery.

It is a marriage of primitive, characteristic antiquity with the latest flourishes of French modernist painting that Diego wants to achieve in his still unfinished work – the murals covering the whole building of the Mexican ministry of public education.

This comprises dozens of walls, depicting the past, the present and the future in the story of Mexico.

Primordial paradise, with its free and easy labour, its time-honoured customs, the festivals of maize, dances of the spirit of death and life, and offerings of fruit and flowers.

Then come the ships of general Hernán Cortés, the conquest and enslavement of Mexico.

Forced labour (all of it at gunpoint), with the planter lounging in a hammock. Frescos showing the work of weaving, casting, pottery and sugar growing. The developing struggle. A gallery of executed revolutionaries. An uprising from the land – attacking even the heavens. The burial of the slain revolutionaries. The liberation of the peasant. The instruction of the peasants under the protection of the armed populace. The union of the workers and the peasants. The construction of the world of the future. The commune – and the flowering of art and learning.

This work was commissioned by the previous short-lived president in the period of his flirtation with the workers.

Now it constitutes the world's first Communist mural – and it's the object of vicious attacks from people in high places, in the government of President Calles.[13]

The United States – Mexico's puppet-master – gave him battleships and cannons, to let it be understood that the Mexican president is merely the instrument of North American capital. And therefore (an easy deduction) there is no need to cultivate Communist agitational painting.

There have been instances of attacks by vandals, and the daubing and scraping of pictures.

That day I had dinner at Diego's.

His wife is a tall beauty from Guadalajara.

We ate purely Mexican things.

Dry, really tasteless, heavy flatcakes or pancakes. Minced meat rolled up in a mass of flour and a whole conflagration of pepper.

Before dinner there was coconut – and afterwards, mango.

This was washed down with cheap vodka with a kick to it like moonshine – a kind of Havana cognac.

Then we repaired to the lounge. In the middle of a divan lolled their one-year-old son, and at the top of it on a cushion apprehensively lay a huge Colt.

I shall provide a few scraps of information about the other arts as well.

POETRY. There's lots of it. In Chapultepec Park there's a whole alley of poets – the *Calzada de los poetas*.

Solitary dreamers scratch away on bits of paper.

One person in every six – just has to be a poet.

But all the questions I put to critics about the significance of today's Mexican poetry, and as to whether there is anything resembling Soviet trends, remained unanswered.

Even the Communist Guerrero, editor of the railway magazine, even the workers' poet Cruz – even they write almost nothing but lyrics about sensuality, full of moans and whispers, and their beloved is liable to be *como un león nubio* ('like a Nubian lion').[14]

The reason, I think, is poetry's weak development, the weak social commission.[15] The editor of *Torch* magazine assured me that you don't pay out fees for verses – what sort of 'work' is that! You only put them in as elegant human posturing, primarily of benefit and interest to the poet alone. It's interesting that this view of poetry existed in Russia too, in the pre-Pushkin and even in the Pushkin period. At that time, it would appear, Pushkin was on his own in being a professional, in putting his poems into his financial statements.

Printed poetry, and for that matter good books in general, do not sell at all. The only exception is translated books. Even a book like *Predatory America*, a seminal book on U.S. imperialism and the possibility of Latin American unification for the struggle, translated and published already in Germany, here sells out in an edition of five hundred copies, and even then only through virtually forcible subscription.

Those who want any circulation for their poetry publish cheap leaflets with a poem adapted for singing to some well-known tune.

I was shown such leaflets by the Peasants' International delegate, comrade Galván. These were pre-election leaflets with his own poems, being sold around the markets for next to nothing. This method ought to be employed by the Proletarian Writers' organisations, rather than printing thick academic anthologies on quality workers' and peasants' paper at five roubles a time.

Russian literature is liked and admired, although largely by hearsay. They are now translating (!) Lev Tolstoy and Chekhov, and of newer things I have only seen Blok's *The Twelve* and my own *Left March*.[16]

THEATRE. Plays, opera and ballet lie fallow. A touring Anna Pavlova[17] would have a full house only if she saw double.

I went one day to a huge theatre to see a puppet show. It was eerie seeing this stunning display brought over from Italy. People, who appeared to be alive, were undergoing fractures in all joints from their contortions. From out of a woman of human size there flew in their dozens tiny dancing dolls of both sexes.

The orchestra and chorus of pint-sized people produced some quite unbelievable *roulades*, and even at this official performance in aid of Mexican airmen only the boxes for diplomatic representatives were full, even though the tickets were quite freely available.

There are two *bataclans*[18] – in imitation of the Parisian nude revue. They are full. The women are skinny and bedraggled. Obviously they are already past it – as regards fashion, age and any success – both in Europe and the States. There is a smell of sweat and scandal. One number, a half-hour of rump rotation, complete with quivering (the other side of the belly-dancing coin) is repeated for the third time – and once again there's a manic whistling, which in Mexico replaces applause.

We also visit the cinema. Mexican cinemas start from eight in the evening and show the one unrepeated programme comprising three or four huge reels.

The content is cowboy, the production American.

But my favourite spectacle of those seen is the bullfight.

A huge steel structure of an arena – the only building built according to all the rules, to an all-American width.

Capacity – about forty thousand. Long before Sunday, the newspapers will announce:

LOS OCHO TOROS
('Eight Bulls')

The bulls and horses taking part in the action can be inspected in advance in the stables for *toros*. All sorts of well-known toreadors, matadors and picadors participate in the festival.

At the appointed hour, thousands of carriages filled with society ladies with their tame monkeys, driving around in their 'Rolls', and tens of thousands of pedestrians push their way towards the steel edifice. The price of the tickets bought up by touts has doubled.

It's an open-air circus.

The aristocrats take their tickets for the shady expensive side, the plebs for the cheap side in the sun. If, after the killing of two bulls, from the overall programme of six or eight, rain forces a cessation on this knacker's yard – as was the case on my visit – all hell breaks loose and a pogrom is launched on the management and any wooden structures.

Then the police wheel up the water cannon and begin to drench the sunlit (plebeian) side with water. This doesn't help – so then they start shooting at these same sunny-siders.

Toros.

In front of the entrance, a huge crowd waits for its favourite bullfighters. Distinguished citizens try to get photographed next to some arrogant bullfighter, aristocratic *señoras* pass them – obviously for their own self-aggrandisement – their children to hold. Photographers muscle in, almost on the bulls' horns – and the bullfight begins.

First there is a splendid parade, full of sparkle. And already the auditorium is starting to go mad, throwing bowler hats, jackets, purses and gloves to their favourites in the arena. The prologue passes off relatively elegantly and calmly, when the toreador teases the bull with a red rag. But from the *banderilleros* on, when they stick the first spears into the bull's neck, when the picadors cut into the bull's side, and the bull turns gradually red, when its maddened horns smash into the horses' bellies, and the picadors' horses tear about momentarily with their guts hanging out – that's when the depraved joy of the auditorium reaches boiling point. I saw one man jump out of his seat, snatch away the toreador's rag and proceed to dangle it in front of the bull's nose.

I then experienced a supreme joy: the bull managed to drive a horn between the man's ribs, taking revenge for his comrade-bulls.

The man was carried out.

No one paid any attention to him.

I could not look, and just didn't want to see, as they presented the sword to the chief murderer and he stuck it into the bull's heart. Only from the rabid uproar in the crowd did I gather that the deed was done. Down below, the skinners were waiting for the carcass with their knives. The only thing I regretted was that it was not possible to mount machine guns on the bull's horns and train him to shoot.

Why should one have to feel sorry for such specimens of humanity?

The one thing that reconciles me to bullfighting is that King Alfonso of Spain is against it.

Bullfighting is the national pride of Mexico.

When, having bid farewell to his vocation, having bought houses and guaranteed food and lackeys for himself and his children, the famous bullfighter Rudolfo Gaona went away to Europe, the country's press howled, and ran surveys. Did this great man have the right to move abroad? Who will the youth of Mexico learn from? Who will be their role model?

I didn't see any impressive architectural landmarks of the new Mexico. The swiftly changing presidents have little time to think about lasting monuments. Díaz, who stuck to the presidency for thirty years, towards the end started to build something halfway between a senate house and a theatre. Díaz[19] was then thrown out. Since then many years have passed. A ready skeleton of iron girders stands there, and just now, it seems, some Mexican speculator is getting it, either for demolition or resale, for services of some sort rendered to the president. One fine new item, I thought, is the Cervantes monument (a copy of the Seville one). A raised area, enclosed by stone benches, with a fountain in the middle – very necessary in the Mexican heat. The benches and the low walls are tiled with slabs, recreating in simple prints the adventures of Don Quixote. A diminutive Don and Sancho Panza stand to the sides. There are no depictions of the moustached or bearded Cervantes.

To make up for this, there are two bookcases of his works, which, for some years now, have been leafed through on the spot by high-minded Mexicans.

THE CITY. Mexico City is flat and multicoloured. From the outside, all the little houses are like boxes. Pink, blue, green. The predominant colour is a pinkish yellow, like sea sand at daybreak. A house's façade is boring – all its beauty is within. Here the house frames a four-cornered courtyard. The court-yard is planted with all kinds of floral tropicality. In front of all the houses, enveloping the courtyard, is a two, three or four-layered terrace, entwined with greenery, covered with pots of creeping plants and parrots' cages.

The whole of the huge American café Samborn was built like this: a glazed roof over a courtyard, and that's all.

This is the Spanish style of housing, brought over here by the conquerors.

Of the ancient eight-hundred-year-old Mexico – when all of this space now taken up by the city was a lake surrounded by volcanoes, and only on a tiny islet stood a pueblo, the original town-dwelling commune of about forty thousand – of this Aztec town, not a trace remained.

On the other hand, there are masses of palaces and houses from the time of Cortés, the initial conqueror of Mexico, from that of the short-lived emperor Iturbide,[20] plus churches and churches, and monasteries. There are far more than ten thousand of them, spread about in Mexico.

And there are huge new cathedrals, from the Notre-Dame lookalike – the cathedral on the Zócalo square – down to the little windowless church in the old town, overgrown with mould and flowers. It was abandoned two hundred years ago, following a battle between the monks and someone or other – and here there's a courtyard where even now lies an antediluvian armament in the same order – or rather disorder – in which it had been abandoned by those defeated in the siege. Bats and swallows drift past the huge books on the wooden stands.

In fact the cathedral just mentioned is little used for prayer. The cathedral has on one side the entrance, and on the other four exits on to four streets. Mexican *señoritas* and *señoritos* make use of the cathedral as a through passage, in order, having left an impression of religious innocence with their waiting chauffeur, to sneak off from the other side into the embraces of a lover, or to walk arm in arm with an admirer.

Although the church lands were confiscated, and religious processions banned by the government, this remains the case only on paper. Actually, the priests apart, religion is observed by a multitude of peculiar organisations: 'The Knights of Columbus', 'The League of Catholic Women', 'The League of Young Catholics' and so on.

These are the houses and the buildings pointed out by the guides and by Cook's:[21] the houses of history – houses of the priests and houses of the rich.

The Communists took me round the areas of poverty, the quarters of the petty apprentices and the unemployed. These dwellings cling together, like the bins on the Sukharevka market, but with even more filth. These lodgings have no windows and through the open doors you can see families of eight or ten crammed together in a single scruffy room.

During the daily summer Mexican rains, water floods over the floors worn down below the pavements and lies there in stinking puddles.

In front of the doors, emaciated titchy children eat boiled maize, sold right there and kept warm under filthy rags that the tradesman himself sleeps on at night.

Grown-ups with at least twelve centimes left in their pocket sit in the *pulquería* – that distinctive Mexican tavern, decorated with serape rugs, with a representation of General Bolívar, with striped ribbons or glass beads instead of doors.

Cactus *pulque*, without food, damages the heart and the stomach. And by the age of forty an Indian will be breathless, and an Indian will have a bulging stomach. And this is a descendant of the likes of the mighty Hawk's Claw, and such hunters of scalps![22] This is a country cleaned out by civilising American imperialists. A country in which, before the discovery of America, the silver that was lying about was not even considered a precious metal. A country in which now you can't even buy a pound of silver, but have to look for it on Wall Street, in New York. American silver; American oil. In the north of Mexico both the dense railway network and the industry, with its up to the minute technology, are under American ownership.

As for the exotica – what the hell use is that! Liana, parrots, tigers and malaria – all that's down in the south; that's for the Mexicans. But – what about the Americans? What, catch tigers and clip their fur for shaving brushes?

Tigers can be left to the Mexicans. That's for them, the exotica of starvation.

The richest country in the world is already firmly planted, by North American imperialism, in this hungry allotment.

Life in the city begins late, at eight or nine o'clock.

The markets open, the metal workshops, the shoemaking and the tailoring shops, all electrified with machine tools for filing and dyeing the heels, with irons for the immediate pressing of a whole suit. Behind the workshops are the government institutions.

The mass of taxis and private cars alternate with the more democratic, rattling, heavy buses that are no more comfortable or capacious than our own conveyancing fleet.

Motor cars compete with buses, and the cars of the various firms compete amongst themselves.

This competition, given the more than passionate character of Spanish drivers, takes on overtly bellicose forms.

Car chases after car, cars together chase after a bus, and all of them together drive onto the pavements, hunting down unthinking pedestrians.

Mexico City is the world's top town – for its number of car accidents.

A driver in Mexico is not held responsible for causing injuries (watch out for yourself!), therefore the average expectation of life without injury is ten years. Once every ten years everyone gets run over. It's true that there are people who may go twenty years without getting run over, but that's at the expense of those who have already been run over within five years.

Unlike the enemies of Mexican humanity – the motor cars – trams fulfil a human role. They ferry the deceased about.

You often see this unlikely spectacle. A tram full of weeping relatives, with the deceased on a catafalque trailer. The whole procession scorches along for all it's worth, with its bell ever clinking, but without any stops.

A weird electrification of death!

Compared to the United States, there are not many people on the streets – little houses have gardens, and the expanse of the city is enormous, but there are only six hundred thousand inhabitants.

There are not many street hoardings. Just at night, one stands out. A Mexican made of electric bulbs throws a lasso out onto a packet of cigarettes. And all the taxis are adorned with a curvaceous swimming woman, advertising bathing costumes.

The only advert popular with the imperturbable Mexican is for the *barato* – a clearance sale. The city is full of these sales. Even the most respectable firms are obliged to announce them – without proclaiming a 'clearance sale', you won't get a Mexican to buy as much as a fig leaf.

In Mexican conditions, this is not a joke. Apparently the municipality put up a notice on one of the town entrance signs into Mexico City, appealing to those Indians overinclined to a state of nature:

Entry Into Mexico City Without Trousers Is Not Allowed

There is exotica in the shops, but it's for the idiots, for tourists buying up souvenirs, for scrawny American women. For their benefit there are jumping beans, glaringly bright serapes which all the donkeys of Guadalajara would shy away from, handbags with printed Aztec calendars, postcards of parrots from real parrot feathers. The Mexican is more likely to stop in front of the machine shops of the Germans, the linen shops of the French, or the furniture shops of the Americans.

There's an endless quantity of foreign enterprises. When, on the French holiday of the Fourteenth of July, the French shops raised their flags, the abundance of them was enough to make you think you were in France.

The greatest commercial sympathy is enjoyed by Germany, the Germans.

They say that a German may travel the length of the land, enjoying universal hospitality, just from love of his nationality.

It's no accident that I saw, in the most popular newspaper here, that typographical machines had recently been delivered, solely German makes, although we are twenty-four hours from America and it's an eighteen-day voyage to Hamburg.

Up until five or six o'clock it's business, work. Then it's off to the swivels. In front of hairdressers' shops in America are these swivels – a glass cylinder with coloured spirals, the standard sign of Mexican barbers. Others go to the shoeshiners. An elongated shop with footstands in front of high stools – and bootblacks for twenty customers.

The Mexican is a bit of a dandy – I've seen workers who use scent. The Mexican woman will go around through the week in rags, so as to dress up in silks on the Sunday. From seven o'clock the central streets blaze with electricity, of which more gets burned here than just about anywhere else – in any case, more than the means of the Mexican people will allow. This amounts to a peculiar form of agitation for vitality and prosperous existence under the incumbent president.

At eleven o'clock, when the theatres and cinemas finish, a few cafés remain open, plus cellar taverns out of town, or on the outskirts – and walking around starts to become not exactly risk-free. Already you can't get into the Chapultepec Park, where the president's palace is.

All over the city there is a rustle of shots. Scurrying police do not always signify a murder. Most commonly shooting takes place in the bars, with a Colt being used as a corkscrew. The necks of bottles are just shot off. Or they just shoot from cars, for the noise. They shoot for bets – they draw lots, to see who will shoot whom – the winner quite legitimately opens fire. In Chapultepec Park the shooting is better thought out. On the president's orders there's no admission to the park from nightfall (the presidential palace being in the park), and shots are to be fired after the third warning. They don't forget to shoot, but they do sometimes forget the warnings. The newspapers report the murders with satisfaction, but without enthusiasm. But, on the other hand, when a day comes to an end without a death, the paper will proclaim: 'No murders today.'

There is a great love for weapons. The ritual for friendly farewells is as follows: you stand stomach to stomach and slap each other on the back. But then again you slap lower down and in the trouser back pocket you will always slap the weighty Colt.

Everyone from the age of fifteen to seventy-five has one.

A DROP OF POLITICS. Just a drop – because that's not my speciality, because I haven't lived in Mexico for long, and because a lot really needs to be written about it.

The political life of Mexico can be considered exotic, because it is at first sight unexpected in its particularities and unusual in its manifestations.

The shuffling of presidents, the decisive voice of the Colt, the never-extinguished revolutions, the fabled bribery, the heroism of the uprisings, the venality of the governments – all of this exists in Mexico, and all of it in abundance.

First of all, on the word 'revolutionary'. In the Mexican sense, this is not only someone who, understanding or guessing at the times to come, fights for this and leads humanity towards it. A Mexican revolutionary is anyone who, weapon in hand, may overthrow the reigning authority – indifferent to whatever it may be.

And since, in Mexico, everyone has either overthrown or is overthrowing, or wants to overthrow the current regime – they are all revolutionaries.

Therefore the word is meaningless in Mexico and so, reading it in the papers as applied to South American life, one has to search further and deeper. I saw many Mexican revolutionaries. These ranged from young Communist enthusiasts, hiding away their Colts for a while, as they wait for Mexico to take the path of our October, to the sixty-five-year-olds amassing millions in order to buy their way just to the starting point from which a presidential post can be imagined.

All in all in Mexico there are around two hundred parties. These can be museum curiosities, such as Rafael Mayén's 'Party of Revolutionary Upbringing', which has an ideology, a programme and a committee, but consists only of him. Or the bankrupt leaders proposing to the city council to lay out at its own expense a whole street, just so that one side street only should be named after them.

From the workers' viewpoint, the 'labouring' party is an interesting one. This is a peaceful 'workers' party', close in spirit to Gompers[23] in North America. This is the best indicator of the way that reformist parties degenerate, replacing revolutionary struggle with jostling for ministerial portfolios, noble speeches from the rostrum and the horse-trading of political intrigue in the corridors.

An interesting figure is the kingpin of this party, the minister of labour, Morones. All the magazines never fail to depict him with diamonds glittering all over his shirt front and sleeves.

Unfortunately, I cannot provide an adequate sketch of the life of the Communists of Mexico.

I lived in Mexico City, the centre of official political life. Working-class life was concentrated more to the north, in the oil centre of Tampico, in the mines of Mexico state, and amongst the peasants of Vera Cruz state. I can only recall a few encounters with comrades.

Comrade Galván, the Mexican representative at the Peasants' International, had organised the first agricultural commune in Vera Cruz, with new tractors and attempts at a new life. He talks about his work like a genuine enthusiast, gives out photographs, and even recites poems about the commune.

Comrade Carío is still very young, but he's one of the best theoreticians of communism – he's their secretary, and treasurer, and editor, and just about everything else, at one and the same time.

Guerrero is an Indian. A Communist artist. A fine political cartoonist – a master of the pencil and the lasso.

Comrade Moreno.[24] Deputy from the state of Vera Cruz.

Moreno wrote in my notebook, having heard 'Left March' (it's a terrible shame that these pages were lost 'in circumstances beyond our control' on the American border):

'Tell the Russian workers and peasants that, for the moment, we are just listening to your march, but the day will come when, after your Mauser, our 33 (a Colt calibre) will also thunder.'

A Colt did thunder, but unfortunately it was not Moreno's – but at Moreno.

When I had already got to New York, I read in a paper that comrade Moreno had been killed by government assassins.

The Mexican Communist party is small; in a proletariat of a million and a half, there are about two thousand Communists – but out of this figure only about three hundred comrades are working activists.

But the Communists' influence is growing and spreading far beyond the limits of the party – the Communist organ *El Machete* has an actual circulation of five thousand.

And one more fact. Comrade Monson became a Communist when he was already in the federal senate, having been sent to the senate by the labourists of the state of San Luis Potosi. Twice his former party summoned him to account – but he didn't appear, occupied with Communist party affairs. Nevertheless, they can't strip him of his position, due to his great popularity among the working masses.

The eccentricity of Mexican politics, the at first sight unusual quality, is explained by the fact that its roots need to be sought not only in the economy of Mexico, but also in the calculations and rapacity of the United States – and, indeed, mainly in those. There are presidents who presided for barely an hour, so that, when the interviewers turned up, the president would already have been dethroned, and would reply with some irritation: 'Don't you know that I was elected for just an hour and a half!'

Such a brisk succession is to be explained, not at all by the lively Spanish temperament, but by the fact that such presidents are chosen by agreement with the States for the speedy and submissive passage of some law or other, defending American interests. Since 1894 (the election of the first president of Mexico, General Guadalupe), over thirty years, the presidency has changed hands thirty-seven times and there have been five radical changes of the constitution. Throw in, too, the fact that, of these thirty-seven, thirty have been generals, meaning that each new investiture was accompanied by the gun, and the volcanic tableau of Mexico will become a little clearer.

And the methods of struggle in Mexico are in accordance with all this.

Before the voting takes place, foreseeing a majority of votes for their opponent, brazen delegates abduct the possessors of the opposing party's extra votes and hold them until the resolution has been carried.

This is not the system, but it happens. One general will invite another one round and, over coffee – sentimental, like all Spaniards – already grasping at his revolver grip, will try to persuade his colleague:

'Drink up, drink up, it's the last cup of coffee of your life.'

It's clear what the end of one of the generals is going to be.

Only in Mexico can there be such incidents as the story of General Blancha, told to me later on, in the American town of Laredo. Blancha was taking towns, in the company of ten associates, by driving down from the mountains a herd of thousands of horses. The population of a town would scatter and surrender, imagining a brigade of thousands, and quite justifiably thinking that horses on their own could not possibly be taking a town. But the horses were taking it, because Blancha was driving them. Blancha was uncatchable, now allying with the Americans against the Mexicans, and now with the Mexicans against the Americans.

They caught him at the women. An enchantress was dispatched to lure him over to the Mexican side, and in a tavern administered to him and his comrade some sort of sleep-inducing muck. They chained him up to his mate and threw the enchained pair into the river that divided the two Laredos, firing at them with their Colts from boats.

Coming to, due to the cold, the gigantic strongman Blancha managed to break off his manacles, but his co-shackled counterpart pulled him down.

Their bodies were only pulled out several days later.

Many ideas are sparked off from these belligerent people, brigades and parties.

But one idea unites everyone. This is the thirst for liberation, a hatred for the enslavers, for the cruel 'gringos', who have made a colony out of Mexico and who have cut off half the territory (so that there are towns, one half of which are Mexican, the other American), for the Americans – a carcass of a hundred and thirty million souls weighing down on a nation of twelve million.

Cachupín and *gringo* – these are the two main swear words in Mexico.

'*Cachupín*' is a Spaniard. Over the five hundred years from the time of the invasion of Cortés, this word has faded, decayed, and lost its acerbity.

But 'gringo' even now rings out like a slap in the face (when they stormed into Mexico, the American troops, they would sing 'Green go the rushes, oh…', the old soldiers' song – and the first words were shortened into the swear word).[25]

An example: a Mexican on crutches. Walking with a woman. The woman is English. There's a passer-by. He looks at the English woman and yells:

'Gringo!'

The Mexican drops his crutch and pulls out his Colt.

'Take back your words, you dog, or I'll drill you on the spot.'

Half an hour of apologies follow, so as to smooth over the appalling, undeserved insult. Of course, in this hatred for the gringo, an exact correspondence between the concepts 'every American' and 'exploiter' is not quite correct. An incorrect and unhealthy understanding of 'nation' has so often paralysed the Mexicans' struggle.

The Mexican Communists know that:

500 poor tribes in the Mexican land,
and the satiated,
a single tongue talk,
squeezing at the lemon with one hand,
locking them in with a single lock.[26]

The workers of Mexico understand more and more that only their comrade Moreno knows where to direct the national hatred, and into which other form of hatred it has to be transferred.

The struggle
can't
cut through to the tribes.
Destitute with destitute,
side by side.

Spread
>> *round the world*
>>> *your Mexican ardour,*
the binding shout:
>> Camarada!

The workers understand more and more (the May Day demonstration is the proof) what has to be done, to make sure that the overthrown American exploiters are not replaced by home-grown ones.

Jettison
>> *from the hump*
>>> *of the pot-bellied your burden,*
Aztec,
>> *Creole*
>>> *and mestizo.*
Swiftly
>> *above the Mexican watermelon,*
crimson flag, up you go!

The Mexican flag is known as the 'watermelon'. There's a legend: a detachment of rebels were thinking about the national colours while stuffing themselves with watermelons.

The necessity for a swift relocation didn't give them long to ruminate.

'Let's make a flag – the watermelon!' decided the detachment, speeding off to battle.

And so it went: green, white, red – outside rind, inside skin, fleshy core.

I left Mexico unwillingly. All the actions I have described so far are carried out by extremely hospitable and extremely pleasant and kind people.

Even the seven-year-old Jesús, running off for my cigarettes, when asked his name, devotedly replied: 'Jesús Pupito, your humble servant.'

A Mexican, giving his address, will never just say: 'this is my address.' A Mexican will inform you: 'now you know where your home is.'

Inviting you to get into his car, he will say: 'I beg you to take a seat in your automobile.'

And letters, not even to an intimate lady friend, will conclude: 'I kiss your footsteps.'

To admire something in someone's house is not possible: it will be wrapped up for you in paper.

The spirit of the unusual, and the cordiality, are what tie me to Mexico.

I want to be in Mexico again, to follow with comrade Khaikis the route planned for us by Moreno: from Mexico City to Vera Cruz, and from there for two days by train to the south, then a day on horseback – and on into the impassable tropical forest, with parrots that won't pick your fortune, and monkeys without waistcoats.[27]

New York

NEW YORK. 'Moscow. That's in Poland?' they asked me at the American consulate in Mexico.

'No,' I replied, 'it's in the U.S.S.R.'

This made no impression.

I was given my visa.

Later I got to know that if an American just has to sharpen the points, then he knows his job better than anyone in the world, but he can never as much as hear anything about the eyes of needles. The needle's eye is not his speciality, and he is not obliged to know about it.

Laredo is the border town with the U.S.A.

I explain for ages in terribly broken (utterly splintered) half-French and half-English the whys and wherefores of my visit.

The American listens, keeps quiet, thinks about it, doesn't understand and, finally, accosts me in Russian:

'You – a yid?'

I was dumbfounded.

The American didn't pursue this conversation any further, for want of additional vocabulary.

He racked his brains, and after about ten minutes he blurted out:

'Greater Russian?'

'Great Russian, yes, Great Russian.' I was relieved to have established in the American a lack of pogrom spirit. His interest was starkly bureaucratic. The American thought it over a bit more and, after another ten-minute interval, passed judgement:

'To the commission.'

One gentleman, appearing to be a civilian passenger up to this moment, put on a peaked cap and turned into an immigration official.

The official bundled me and my things into a car. We drove up to, and went into, a building, in which a man without a jacket or a waistcoat was sitting under a starry flag.

Behind the man there were other rooms which had bars. I and my things were accommodated in one of these.

I tried leaving, but precautionary paws drove me back.

Not far away, my New York train whistled.

I was sitting there for four hours.

They came in, wanting to know in what language I would be explaining myself.

Out of pure abashment (it is embarrassing not knowing any one foreign language) I nominated French.

I was taken into a room.

Four menacing types and a French interpreter.

I'm fine with simple French conversations about tea and buns, but, out of the phrases said to me by the Frenchman I understood not a thing, and just seized frantically on the final word, trying intuitively to pierce the hidden sense.

While I was still piercing, the Frenchman guessed that I didn't understand a thing; the Americans waved their arms about and I was taken back again.

Sitting there for another two hours, I found in the dictionary the Frenchman's final word.

It turned out that it was: 'oath'.

Swearing an oath in French was beyond me, and therefore I had to wait for them to find a Russian.

After two hours the Frenchman came in and excitedly re-assured me:

'They've found a Russian. *Bon garçon.*'

The same guys. The interpreter this time an emaciated, phlegmatic Jew, the proprietor of a furniture shop.

'I need to take an oath,' I faltered timidly, so as to start a conversation.

The interpreter gave an indifferent wave of his hand:

'Well, you'll be telling the truth, if you don't prefer to lie, and if you do want to lie, then you won't tell the truth anyway.'

The view of reason.

I began answering hundreds of bureaucratic questions: my mother's maiden name, my grandfather's origins, the address of my secondary school, and so on. Things I had completely forgotten about!

The interpreter turned out to be a man of influence and, having once got stuck into the Russian language, I quite understandably made a favourable impression on him.

To cut it short, they let me into the country for six months, as a tourist, under an indemnity of five hundred dollars.

Within just half an hour the whole Russian colony had rushed down to have a look at me, falling over themselves with offers of hospitality.

The owner of a small shoe shop, making me sit on a low chair for fittings, demonstrated the fashions in shoes, produced some ice-cold water, and rejoiced:

'The first Russian for three years! Three years ago a priest came through with his daughters. At first he cut up rough, but then (after I'd fixed it for his two daughters to dance in the *café chantant*) he said: "Although you're a yid, you're a decent sort – you must be well meaning, since you did a priest a good turn."'

Then I got caught by a retailer who sold me two shirts at two dollars each at cost price (one dollar for the shirt and another for the friendship), and then he was so moved that he took me across the whole town to his house and made me drink warm whiskey out of his only tooth-mug – which was stained and reeking of mouthwash.

My first encounter with the American dry anti-drink laws – 'prohibition'. Then I came back to the interpreter's furniture shop. His brother undid the price tag on the very best plush green divan in the shop, and he sat down himself on another one opposite, a leather one with a tag of $99.95 (a commercial ruse, so it wouldn't be 'a hundred').

At that point a quartet of miserable-looking Jews came in: two young women and two young men.

'Spaniards,' says the brother, introducing them disapprovingly, 'from Vinnitsa and Odessa. Two years they spent, sitting around in Cuba, waiting for their visas. In the end they entrusted themselves to an Argentinian' – who saw them across for two hundred and fifty dollars.

The Argentinian was a solid citizen and, going by his passport, he had four children who were travelling with him. Argentinians don't need visas. The Argentinian had brought about four hundred or six hundred children over to the United States – and now had got caught with the six hundred and fourth.

This Hispanic type is well settled. Some unknown people have already put a hundred thousand dollars in the bank for him – so he must be quite someone.

And the brother was standing bail for this lot, but it wouldn't do any good – the trial will go ahead and they'll be deported anyway.

This man was a big entrepreneur, too – and an honest one. But there are lots of petty operators here as well. At a hundred dollars a time they undertake to ferry people over from the Mexican to the American Laredo. They pocket the hundred, take them out to the middle, and then drown them.

Many have done their emigrating straight to the other world.

This is my last tale of Mexico.

The tale of the brother about his brother, the furniture man, is my first American one. The brother had lived in Kishinev. When he got to fourteen, he found out from rumours that the most beautiful women are to be found in Spain. The brother ran away that very evening, because he really needed the most beautiful women. But he got to Madrid only when he reached seventeen. In Madrid, as it turned out, there were no more beautiful women than there were everywhere else, and they would look at the brother even less than the chemists' shop assistants in Kishinev had done. The brother took offence and quite rightly decided that, to attract the sparkle of Spanish eyes in his direction, he had to have money. The brother went off to America with two other vagrants – but, at least, with one pair of shoes for all three of them. He got on a ship, but not on the one he needed to be on, but on the one he managed to get on. On his arrival, America unexpectedly proved to be England, and by mistake the brother found himself stuck in London. In London the unshod trio collected cigarette ends, the hungry trio made new cigarettes out of the fag-end tobacco, and then one of them (taking it in turns), sporting the shoes, went selling them along the embankment. Within a few months, their tobacco commerce extended beyond these butt-end cigarettes, their horizons extended to some comprehension of the whereabouts of America, and their well-being stretched to shoes of their own and a third-class ticket to somewhere called Brazil. On the voyage out, the brother won a certain sum at cards. In Brazil, through commerce and gambling, he increased this sum to thousands of dollars.

Then, taking the lot with him, the brother went off to the races, committing all his cash to the tote. The inconsiderate mare lagged at the rear, showing little concern at impoverishing the brother in thirty-seven seconds flat. A year later, the brother skipped it to Argentina and bought a bicycle, having conceived a lasting contempt for nature's creatures.

Having acquired the art of bicycle riding, the irrepressible man from Kishinev got himself involved in cycle racing.

So as to come first, a brief sortie onto the pavement had to be made – the minute was gained, but by pure chance a gaping old woman was knocked into a ditch by the speed merchant.

The result of this was that the entire considerable first prize had to be given over to the dishevelled granny.

Out of pique, the brother went off to Mexico, where he hit on the obvious law of colonial commerce: a mark-up of three hundred per cent – a hundred per cent for credulity, a hundred per cent for expenses, and a hundred per cent for the extra rip-off in the instalment payments.

Having once again put a certain bit aside, over he went to the American side, where any form of profiteering is encouraged.

Here the brother isn't bogged down in any particular business. He buys a soap-works for six thousand and sells it for nine. He acquires a shop and then gets rid of it, smelling a crash a month in advance. Now he is a highly esteemed personage of the town: he's the president of dozens of charities; when Pavlova passed through, he paid out three hundred dollars for one dinner.

'Here he is!' the excited raconteur pointed up the street. The brother was belting along in a new car, trying it out; he was selling his own car for seven and snapping up this one for twelve.

A man was standing obsequiously on the pavement, smiling in such a way that anyone could see his gold crowns, his eyes flashing eagerly in pursuit of this car.

'That's a young haberdasher,' it was explained to me. 'He and his brother have been here four years in all, and he's already been twice to Chicago on business. But his brother is hopeless, a Greek of some sort, just writes poetry all the time. He's got himself fixed up as a teacher in the next town, but all the same, he'll get nowhere.'

In his delight at meeting a Russian, my new friend conducted me around the streets of Laredo in a mood of fantastic cordiality.

He ran on in front of me, opening doors, fed me with an extended lunch, agonised at the merest hint of any payment on my part, took me to the cinema, looking all the time at me and rejoicing whenever I laughed – all this without the least notion of anything about me, other than for the single word 'Muscovite'.

We walked to the railway station along dark empty streets, along which, as always in the provinces, free administrative fantasy had got carried away.

On the asphalt (a thing I never saw, even in New York) white stripes indicated exactly where citizens should cross, great white arrows directed the non-existent crowds and traffic, and for an unapproved crossing of deserted streets a fine of getting on for fifty roubles was levied. At the station I grasped the full omnipotence of the furniture shop brother. From Laredo to San Antonio they wake the passengers up the whole night long, checking passports in the hunt for border-crossers devoid of visas. But I was presented to the commissioner and so I slept soundly through my first American night, infusing respect in the Negroes sleeping in the Pullman car.

In the morning, America rolled past, the express whistled, without stopping, sucking in water through its proboscis as it went.

All around there are well-kept roads crawling with Fords, and various structures of the technological fantasy-land. Around the railway halts could be seen Texas cowboy houses with fine mosquito netting on the windows and with divan-like hammocks on the spacious terraces. Stone-built stations were divided exactly into two halves: half for us, the whites, and half for the blacks – 'For Negroes' – with its own wooden chairs and its own ticket office – and woe and betide, should you even accidentally fetch up on the other side!

Trains rushed on ever further. From the right side a plane was soaring, flew over to the left, zoomed up again having whizzed over the train, and skimmed along again on the right.

This was one of the American border-guard patrol planes.

By the way, these were almost the only ones I saw in the United States.

The next ones I saw were only those in the three-day air-racing events in a night-time publicity campaign over New York.

Strangely enough, aviation here is relatively undeveloped.

The mighty railway companies even relish every air crash, and exploit these for anti-flying propaganda.

That was the case with the airship Shenandoah, which broke in half (during my stay in New York), when thirteen people were saved, but seventeen were smashed into the ground, together with the heap of outer casing and steel cables.

And so, in the United States, there are virtually no passenger flights.

Perhaps only now are we on the eve of airborne America. Ford launched his first aeroplane and installed it in Wanamaker's department store in New York – in the place where, many years back, the first Ford car had been shown off.

New Yorkers clamber into its cabin, tug its tail, stroke its wings – but the price of twenty-five thousand dollars repels the general consumer. And in the mean while, planes were flying up to San Antonio, and then the real American towns started. There was a flash of the American Volga – the Mississippi; I was taken aback by the train station in St Louis; and, in shafts of light from the twenty-storey skyscrapers of Philadelphia, there shone, like virgin soil, what, in broad daylight, is the inordinate extravagance of electrical advertising.

This was just a practice start, so that New York shouldn't surprise me. Much as the entangled nature of Mexico can amaze, with its plants and its people, New York, surfacing from the ocean with its piled-high buildings and its technological achievement, will completely flabbergast you. I had travelled into New York from dry land, and had stuck my nose into no more than one train station, but, notwithstanding three days training on the journey from Texas, my eyes were still out on stalks.

For hours the train tears along the bank of the Hudson, at about two paces from the water. On the other side there are more roads, right at the foot of the Bear Mountains. Loads of boats and small craft are pushing along. More and more bridges seem to leap across the train. The carriage windows are increasingly being filled with the upright walls of maritime docks, coal depots, electrical placements, steel foundries and pharmaceutical works. An hour before the terminus, you pass through a continuous density of chimneys, roofs, two-storey walls, and the steel girders of an elevated railway. With every step of the way, the roofs grow an extra floor. Eventually, tenements loom up, with their shaftlike walls and windows in squares, tinier squares and dots. Never mind how far back you crane your head, you can't see the top of them. This makes everything even more cramped, as though you were rubbing your cheek against this stone. Completely lost, you sink back onto your seat – there's no hope, your eyes are just not used to this sort of thing; then you come to a stop – it's Pennsylvania Station.

There's no one, except for the Negro porters, on the platform. There are lifts and steps going up. Up above, there are several tiers of galleries and balconies, with lots of handkerchief-wavers greeting people, or seeing them off.

Americans keep quiet (or, perhaps, people only seem like that against the roar of the machinery), but over American heads megaphones and loudspeakers drone on about arrivals and departures.

Electric power is further utilised twofold and threefold by the white plates covering the windowless galleries and walkways, broken by information points, whole rows of commercial cash tills, and all kinds of shops that never close – from ice cream parlours and snack bars to crockery and furniture stores.

It is hardly conceivable that anyone could clearly imagine this whole labyrinth in its entirety. If you have come in for business at an office say two miles away downtown, in the banking or business sector of New York, on maybe the fifty-third floor of the Woolworth Building, and you have owlish proclivities – there's no need for you even to emerge from underground. Right here, under the ground, you get into a station lift and it will whizz you up to the vestibule of the Pennsylvania Hotel, a hotel of two thousand guest-rooms of all conceivable types.

Everything a visiting businessman can need: post offices, banks, telegraph offices, all sorts of goods – you'll find everything here, without even going outside the hotel.

This is where a few rather clever mothers will sit, with their only too obvious daughters.

Go dancing.

Noise and tobacco smoke. Like the eagerly awaited interval in a huge theatre during a long and tedious play.

That same lift will take you down below ground (to the 'subway'), you take the express, and this will rip through the miles even better than a train. Out you get, at the building you want. A lift whisks you up to the required floor without any exits on to the street. By the same route, you can get back to the station, under the celestial ceiling of Pennsylvania Station, under the blue sky, from which the Great Bear, Capricorn and other constellations are already glittering.[28] And the more reserved American can travel home, in trains that leave by the minute, to his out-of-town rocking-settee, without as much as a backward glance at the Sodom and Gomorrah of New York City.

Even more striking is Grand Central Station, which towers over several blocks.

The train skims through the air at a height of three or four storeys. The smoky steam engine is replaced by a clean, non-spluttering electric one – and the train plunges underground. For a quarter of an hour there will still flash below you the green-entwined railings – chinks of quiet, aristocratic Park Avenue. Then this too finishes and there stretches out half an hour of subterranean city with thousands of arches and black tunnels, streaked with gleaming rails: every roar, thump and whistle pulsates and hangs on for quite some time. The gleaming white rails go yellowish, then red, and then green from the changing colours of the signals. In all directions, there seems to be a tangle of trains, choked with arches. They say that our emigrants, arriving from the placid Russian quarter in Canada, at first cling dumbfoundedly to the window, and then start whooping and lamenting: 'We've had it, mates, we're being buried alive! How can we get out of this?'

We arrive.

Above us are layers of station premises; below the waiting rooms are floors of offices; all around, the boundless iron of the tracks; and beneath us too the underground three-storey subway.

In one of his *Pravda* feuilletons, comrade Pomorsky sceptically derided the stations of New York, counterposing the example of those Berlin coops, the Zoo and Friedrichstrasse.

I don't know what personal accounts comrade Pomorsky may have to settle with the stations of New York. Neither do I know all the technical details, facilities and capacities. But outwardly, cityscape-wise, in terms of urban stimulation, New York's railway stations are one of the most imperious sights in the world.

I love New York on busy autumn days, in the working week.

Six in the morning. Thunder and rain. It's dark, and it'll stay dark until midday.

You get dressed thanks to electricity, on the streets there is electricity, the buildings are bathed in electricity; the evenly chiselled windows are like a stencilled advertising poster. With the inordinate length of the buildings, and the winking colours of the traffic controls, all the motions are doubled, tripled and magnified tenfold by the asphalt – which has been licked as clean as a mirror by the rain. In the narrow chasms between the buildings, a kind of adventurist wind hums through the chimneys, tears down signs and grumbles around them, attempts to knock you off your feet, and then flees, unpunished and uncaught, for miles through the ten avenues that slice across Manhattan (New York's island) from the ocean to the Hudson. From the sides, numerous minor tones from the narrow side streets howl in accompaniment to the storm, just as evenly cutting their swathes across Manhattan – from the one water's edge to the other. Under awnings – and on a rainless day, straight on the pavements – fresh newspapers lie about in heaps, having been delivered earlier by lorries and slung around here by the paper-sellers.

Around the small cafés, single men start getting their body machinery into gear, cramming the first fuel of the day into their mouths – a hurried cup of rotten coffee and a baked bagel, which right here, in samples running to hundreds, the bagel-making machine is slinging into a cauldron of boiling and spitting fat.

Down below, there flows a stream of humanity. At first, before dawn, there is a black-purplish mass of Negroes, who carry out the most arduous and dismal tasks. Then, towards seven, it's an uninterrupted flow of whites. On they go, in the one direction in their hundreds of thousands, to their places of work. But their resinated yellow waterproofs sizzle and glitter like innumerable samovars in the electric light – running wet, yet inextinguishable, even under this rain.

There are still almost no motor cars or taxis.

The crowd flows along, inundating the apertures to the underground, protruding into the covered thoroughfares to the airborne trains, and racing through the air at a height in double- and triple-decker parallel overhead trains. The fast trains run almost without stops, while the local ones make stops every five blocks.

These five parallel train lines fly at a height of three storeys along five avenues, and by 120th Street they scramble up to a height of eight or nine storeys – and lifts then bring up a new lot, coming straight from the squares and streets. There are no tickets. You drop into a tall bollard-like cash machine a five-cent coin, which, to avert fraud, is magnified on the spot and viewed by the attendant sitting in the booth.

Five cents – and you can travel any distance, but in the one direction.

The girders and the roofs of the elevated railways often amount to a continuous awning, running the whole length of a street, and you can see neither the sky nor the houses to the side. There is just the thundering of the trains above your head, and the thundering of the heavy traffic in front of your nose – chunterings, of which you really can't make out as much as a word. In order not to lose the art of moving your lips, it only remains to chew silently the American cud – chewing gum.

A stormy morning is the best time of all in New York – when there isn't a single loafer, not a spare person about. There are only the toilers of the great army of labour of the city of ten million.

The working masses melt away into the gents' and ladies' clothing factories, into the underground tunnels being newly excavated, to their infinite occupations at the port. By eight o'clock, the streets fill up with immeasurable numbers of the cleaner and better-groomed, with an overwhelming smack of bobbed, bare-kneed, lean girls with sinuous stockings – the workforce of the clerical offices, the businesses and the shops. They get scattered through all the floors of the downtown skyscrapers, around the side corridors fed by the main entrance of dozens of lifts.

There are dozens of lifts for local connections, stopping at every floor, and dozens of express lifts, going up without a stop until the seventeenth, the twentieth, or the thirtieth. Special clocks show you what floor the lift is now on, lights indicating, in red and white, descent or ascent.

And if you have two calls to make – one on the seventh floor and another on the twenty-fourth – you take the local up to the seventh, and then, so as not to waste six whole minutes, you change to the express.

Up until one o'clock, typewriters chatter, jacketless people sweat, columns of figures lengthen on paper.

If an office is what you need, then there's no reason to rack your brains over establishing it.

You phone up to some thirtieth floor set-up:

'Hello! Fix me up a six-room office for tomorrow. I want twelve typists for it. And a sign: "The Great Famous Compressed Air Company for Pacific Ocean Submarines". Two boys in brown livery – caps with starred ribbons – and twelve thousand forms, headed as above.'

'Goodbye.'

The next day, you can walk into your office, and your telephone boys will greet you effusively.

'How do you do, Mr Mayakovsky.'

At one o'clock comes a break: an hour for the office workers, and fifteen minutes for the labourers.

Lunch.

Everyone's lunch is dependent on the weekly wage. The fifteen-dollar people buy a dry snack in a paper bag for a nickel and munch away with the full zest of youth.

The thirty-five-a-week lot go to a huge mechanised eating point. Having shoved in their five cents, they press a knob, and an exactly measured quantity of coffee splashes out into a cup. And for another two or three nickels they can open one of the little glass doors to the sandwiches on the huge shelves piled with comestibles.

The sixty-dollar types eat grey pancakes with golden syrup and eggs around the countless Childses-Rockefeller cafés – as white as any bathroom.

The hundred-dollar-and-plus people go to restaurants of all the nationalities – Chinese, Russian, Assyrian, French, Hindu – anywhere except tasteless American ones which guarantee you gastritis with Armour tinned meat that's been lying around almost since the War of Independence.

The hundred-dollar people take their time eating – they can be late back to work – and after they have left, eighty-proof whiskey flasks (brought to help things along) are lying about under the table. Another glass or silver flask, flat and in a form easier against the hip, rests in the back pocket – a weapon of love and friendship on a par with the Mexican Colt.

How does the labourer eat?

The labourer eats poorly.

I didn't see many of them, but those I did see, even those who were well paid, can only manage, in their fifteen-minute break, a quick bite of their dry snack by their machinery, or in front of the factory wall, on the street.

Labour laws requiring the provision of eating space at work have not yet got as far as the United States.

You will search New York in vain for the caricatured organisation, orderliness, rapidity and composure so glorified in literature.

You will see crowds of people loafing around the streets with nothing to do. They will all stop and talk to you about any subject. If you raise your eyes to the heavens and stand still for a minute, you will be surrounded by a mob which a policeman would be hard put to disperse. Their capacity for entertaining themselves with something beyond the stock market goes a long way towards reconciling me to the crowds of New York.

Then it's work again, until five, six, or seven in the evening.

From five until seven is the most boisterous, the most congested time.

To those who have finished work, there can also be added the shoppers, male and female, and simply the *flâneurs*.

On the most crowded street, Fifth Avenue, which cuts the city in half, from the height of the upstairs of the hundreds of trundling buses, you can see tens of thousands of cars, racing in six or eight lanes in either direction. Drenched in the rain that had just fallen, they are now gleaming with a lacquer finish.

Every two minutes, the green lights of the numerous traffic signals go off, and the red lights come on.

Then the motor car and human flood is paralysed for two minutes, so as to let through those tearing out from the side streets.

Within two minutes, the green signal again lights up on the traffic lights, while the side roads are barred by the red lights on the street corners.

Fifty minutes is needed at this time of day for a journey that in the morning would take a quarter of an hour, and pedestrians have to stand and wait for two minutes, deprived of any hope of an immediate crossing.

When you are on the late side running across, and you can see an automobile avalanche breaking away from the chain of its two-minute halt, you might – having forgotten about all your convictions – hide under the wing of a policeman. Or what you might call a wing: in actual fact, it will be the strong arm of one of the loftiest people of New York, with a very weighty stick – a club.

This stick is not always used just for regulating this outlandish traffic. Sometimes (as during a demonstration) it's the means of stopping you in your tracks. A good clout on the back of the head and you don't know whether you're in New York or in tsarist Belostok – or so my friends have told me.

From about six or seven, Broadway lights up – my very favourite street, the only one that capriciously and brazenly butts through streets and avenues as regular as prison bars. It's harder to get lost in New York than it is in Tula. From north to south run the avenues, and from east to west the streets. Fifth Avenue divides the city in half, between West and East. And that's all there is to it. I'm on Eighth Street, on the corner of Fifth Avenue. I want to get to the Fifty-third Street and Second Avenue corner. That means I have to go forty-five blocks, and turn right to the corner of Second.

Of course, not the whole of the twenty-mile-long Broadway is lit up (here you wouldn't say: 'call in, we're neighbours, we both live on Broadway') – just the stretch from Twenty-fifth to Fiftieth Street, and especially Times Square. This, as the Americans say, is the Great White Way.

It really is white, and there really is a feeling that it's brighter than day on it, since it's light all day, but this road is as bright as day and, what's more, it's against the background of darkest night. The light of the street lamps, the light of the darting advertisements, the light of the glowing window displays and the window panes of the never-closing shops, the light from lamps illuminating the huge daubed posters, the light bursting out from the doors of cinemas and theatres as they open, the racing light from the cars and elevated transport, the light from underground trains flashing under your feet in the window panes along the pavements, the light of publicity messages in the sky.

Light, light and light.

You can read a newspaper, and what's more you can read your neighbour's – and in a foreign language, too.

It's bright in the restaurants and in the theatre centre.

It's clean on the main streets and in the places where the bosses or the aspiring bosses live.

Over there, where most of the labourers and junior office workers get conveyed back to, in the poorer Jewish, Negro and Italian quarters on Second and Third Avenues, between First and Thirtieth Streets – the filth is even better than you get in Minsk. And in Minsk it's particularly filthy.

Bins filled with every kind of garbage stand there, and from these the poverty-stricken pick out any not entirely nibbled bones and pieces. Stinking puddles from today's and the day before yesterday's rain lie there cooling.

Litter and putrefaction lie about ankle-deep – not just figuratively ankle-deep, but literally and for real.

And this is within a fifteen-minute stroll, or a five-minute ride, of sparkling Fifth Avenue and Broadway.

The closer you get to the docks, the darker, filthier and more dangerous it gets.

In the daytime, this is an extremely interesting area. Something always has to be crashing about here – whether it's the work going on, or shots, or shouting. Cranes make the earth shudder, unloading some ship, as they drag out almost an entire house by the chimney from the hold.

Strike pickets are there, not allowing any strike-breakers through.

Today, the 10th of September,[29] the New York port seamen's union has declared a strike in solidarity with the striking seamen of England, Australia and South Africa, and on the very first day the unloading of thirty huge ships has been halted.

The day before yesterday, in spite of the strike situation, the rich lawyer and leader of the Socialist Party (the equivalent here of the Mensheviks) Morris Hillquit arrived on the steamship *Majestic*, brought over by strike-breakers. Thousands of Communists and I. W. W.[30] members whistled at him from the shore and threw rotten eggs.

In another few days, they shot at a general who was arriving for some congress or other – the suppressor of Ireland – and he had to be led out by the back way.[31]

But in the morning once again the *La France*, the *Aquitania*, and other fifty-thousand-ton giants sail in and are unloaded along the numerous docks of the numerous companies.

The avenues adjacent to the quays are known here as the 'Avenues of Death' – because of the locomotives pulling in with their goods right onto the street, and because of the villains who pack the pubs.

It is from here that robbers and hold-up specialists are supplied for the whole of New York: to the hotels, to put whole families to the slaughter for a few dollars; and to the subway, where they thrust cashiers into the corner of their change booths and snatch the day's takings, at the same time changing the dollar bills of the unsuspecting public passing through.

If they get caught, it's the electric chair at Sing Sing jail. But it's also possible for them to get away with it. On his way to rob, a bandit might call in on his lawyer and say:

'Phone me, sir, at such and such a time and such and such a place. If I'm not there, that means I'll be needing bail and release from custody.'

Bail sums are considerable, but the criminals are not just petty thieves and are quite well organised.

It turned out, for instance, that a house valued at two hundred thousand dollars was already being used as surety of two million settled on various crooks.

In the papers there were reports of one criminal who had got out of prison on bail forty-two times. Here, on the Avenue of Death, the Irish run the show. In other areas, it will be others.

Negroes, Chinese, Germans, Jews, Russians – they all live in their own districts, with their own customs and language, preserving these through the decades in unadulterated purity.

In New York City, not counting the suburbs, there are one million and seven hundred thousand Jews (roughly).

A million Italians.

Half a million Germans.

Three hundred thousand Irish.

Three hundred thousand Russians.

A quarter of a million Negroes.

A hundred and fifty thousand Poles.

Three hundred thousand Spaniards, Chinese and Finns.

An enigmatic picture: who then, essentially, are the Americans, and how many of them are hundred per cent American?

At first I made manic efforts to manage to speak English inside a month. Just as my efforts were beginning to make some headway, the near-at-hand (or even near-at-foot, or to boot) shopkeeper, milkman, laundryman, and even the policeman – they all began speaking to me in Russian.

Returning at night on the elevated train, you can see these nationalities and districts as though they were cut in slices: on 125th Street the Negroes stand up to get off, on Ninetieth the Russians, on Fiftieth the Germans, and so on, almost precisely.

At midnight, those coming out of the theatres drink a last soda, eat a last ice cream, and crawl home at one, or at three, should they hang about for a couple of hours foxtrotting, or in the final yelling of 'Charleston'. But life does not come to a stop. In the same way, shops of all sorts are open, the subway and the elevated are still running, you can still find a cinema which will stay open all night, and sleep there as long as you like for your twenty-five cents.

Getting home, if it's spring or summer, you close the windows to keep out mosquitoes and gnats, you wash out your ears and your nostrils, and cough up the coal dust. Especially just now, when a four-month strike by 158,000 miners of solid coal has deprived the city of anthracite, and the factory chimneys belch out smoke from soft coal, the use of which is normally forbidden in the big cities.

If you've got a scratch, deluge yourself in iodine: the New York air is chock full of all kinds of muck that will make sties grow, and cause any scratches to swell up and fester. It's the air that is lived off by millions who have nothing and are unable to go away anywhere.

I HATE NEW YORK ON A SUNDAY. At about ten o'clock, some office worker opposite, dressed only in lilac underwear, raises his blinds. Without, it would seem, putting on his trousers, he sits down at the window with his hundred-page edition of either the *World* or the *Times*, weighing two pounds. He'll read for an hour first the poetic and colourful section of big-store publicity (which forms the basis of the average American world outlook), and after the adverts he'll have a glance at the burglary and murder pages.

Then the man puts on his jacket and trousers, from which his shirt will always be hanging out. Under his chin is tightened a permanently knotted tie – of a colour like a cross between a canary, a fire and the Black Sea. Fully dressed, the American will aim to sit for about an hour with the hotel owner, or with the doorman, on chairs on the low steps that go round the house, or on the seats in the nearest bare little garden square.

The conversation concentrates on who has visited whom at night, whether anything has been heard of any drinking, and –

were there to have been visiting and drinking – shouldn't those concerned be reported, with the objective of their eviction and prosecution as adulterers and drunkards.

By one o'clock the American goes off to lunch, to where people richer than he go for lunch, and where his good lady will go into raptures over a fatted fowl at seventeen dollars. After this, the American will go for the hundredth time to the tomb of General Grant and of Mrs General Grant, which is festooned with coloured glass. Or, having divested himself of boots and jacket, he will lie, in some garden square, on a previously read spread from the *Times*, bequeathing to society and the city his scraps of newspaper, a chewing gum wrapper and an area of trampled grass.

Those who are richer are still working up their appetite for lunch, cruising around in their cars, sailing scornfully past the cheaper cars, and blinking jealously at the more luxurious and expensive models.

Particular envy is, of course, aroused in Americans – who aren't particularly blue-blooded – by those who can boast the small golden crown of a baron or a count on their car doors.

If an American is in a car with a lady who has dined out with him, he will kiss her straight away and demand that she kiss him back. Without this 'token of gratitude', he will consider the dollars spent on the bill as money down the drain, and will never go anywhere again with this ungrateful lady. And the lady herself will be scoffed at by her sagacious and thrifty lady friends.

If an American is motoring on his own, he (the paragon of morality and chastity) will slow down and stop beside every solitary pretty female pedestrian, bare his teeth in a big smile, and tempt her into his car with a wild roll of the eyes. A lady who fails to appreciate his passion will qualify as an idiot who doesn't realise how lucky she is to have the opportunity of getting to know the owner of this 100-horse-power motor car.

However, it would be ludicrous to regard this gentleman as a sporting type. Probably, he is able only to drive (that's the least of it), and in the event of a breakdown wouldn't even know how to pump up a tyre or put up the jack. And that's hardly surprising, when this will be done for him in the innumerable garages and petrol stations on every route he ever takes.

In general terms, I am not a great believer in American sportsmanship.

In the main, it's the idle rich who take up sport.

It's true that President Coolidge,[32] even when he's travelling, receives hourly telegraphed updates on the progress of baseball matches between the Pittsburgh team and the Washington team (the Senators). It's true that you get more people in front of bulletins put up on the progress of football games than you would, in another country, in front of a map of military movements in a war that had just started. But this is not a sporting interest, it's the unhealthy interest of the ardent gambler who has bet his bottom dollar on this team or that one.

And if the footballers watched by seventy thousand people in the huge New York arena are hefty and robust, then the seventy thousand spectators, most of them, are a feeble and weak-kneed lot, among whom I look like a Goliath.

The same impression is also left by American soldiers, except for the recruiting sergeants, who sing the praises of a free and easy soldierly life in front of the posters. It was not without reason, in the last war, that these fine fastidious fellows refused to get into a French goods train (forty men or eight horses per wagon), and demanded a soft-seated passenger coach.

At five o'clock the motorists and the wealthier and more refined of the pedestrians race off to their fashionable or less fashionable 'five o'clocks'. The host will have stocked up with bottles of 'sailor gin' and 'ginger ale', and this cocktail gives you the American champagne of the prohibition era.

Girls arrive in their roll-on stockings – shorthand typists and models.

The young arrivals and their host, attracted by a thirst for lyric poetry, but with little grasp of its nuances, utter quips that would turn even a crimson Easter egg red; and, having lost their conversational thread, they'll slap a lady on the thigh as spontaneously as an absent-minded speaker will rap his cigarette case with a cigarette.

The ladies show off their knees and mentally weigh up how much this man is worth.

So that the five o'clock should have a chaste and artistic character, the men will play poker or examine their host's latest acquisitions in ties and braces.

Then they will disperse homeward. After a change of clothes, they will set off for dinner.

The slightly poorer people (not poor, but slightly poorer) eat rather better, the rich rather worse. The slightly poorer eat freshly bought food at home; they eat by electric light, as though taking full cognisance of what they are swallowing.

The slightly richer dine in expensive restaurants on peppered-up out-of-date food that is either going off, or tinned. They eat in semi-darkness, preferring candles to electricity.

These candles make me laugh.

All the electricity belongs to the bourgeoisie, yet they eat by candle-end.

They have an unconscious fear of their own electricity.

They are embarrassed, like the sorcerer who has called up spirits he is unable to control.

This is the very same attitude that most of the people have to the rest of their technology.

Having invented the gramophone and the radio, they throw these to the 'plebs' (as they contemptuously say) and they themselves go and listen to Rachmaninov,[33] whom they mostly don't understand. But they give him the freedom of some city or other, and present him with a golden casket of shares in some sewerage company – to the tune of forty thousand dollars.

Having invented cinema, they throw this to the hoi polloi, and they themselves fight over season tickets to the opera, where the wife of the industrialist McCormick, who possesses a dollar fortune sufficient to do anything she can wish for, yells away like a white whale, lacerating your ears.[34] And should the opera-house flunkeys not keep their eyes peeled, she gets pelted with rotten apples and putrid eggs.

And even when 'society' types do go to the cinema, they will tell you barefaced lies about being at the ballet, or a nude review.

The billionaires escape from a Fifth Avenue that is polluted by traffic noise and ravaged by crowds – they escape out of town, to the still quiet country-house areas.

'Well, I can't possibly live here,' declared a capricious Miss Vanderbilt, selling off her palatial residence on the corner of Fifth Avenue and Fifty-third Street for six million dollars. 'I can't live here, when there's Childs opposite, there's a bakery to the right, and a hairdresser's on the left.'

After dinner, for the well-off, it's theatres, concerts and revues, where a ticket to look at naked ladies from the front row costs ten dollars. For the idiots, it's a trip in a car adorned with fancy lights to Chinatown, where they will be shown perfectly ordinary blocks and houses, in which absolutely ordinary tea is drunk – only not by Americans, but by the Chinese.

For the less well-off couples, there's a capacious bus to Coney Island – the Island of Entertainment. After a long drive, you find yourself amid unbroken Russian (though in Russia we call them American) mountains,[35] sky-high wheels hoisting up their cages, Tahitian kiosks with dancing and a photograph of the island as a background, wheels of death scattering those who step on, bathing pools, and donkey rides. And all this is bathed in such electric illumination that the most brilliant Paris international exhibition couldn't get within spitting distance of it.

In separate stalls, all the most repulsive human freaks in the world have been collected – a bearded woman, a birdman, a woman with three legs, and so on – creatures that stimulate in the Americans an all too sincere delight.

Here too is a constantly changing supply of hungry women, who can be hired for cents, to be shoved into a box for a demonstration of the art of painless puncturing with swords. Others are seated on a chair equipped with levers, and they get electrified until showers of sparks are discharged from extraneous personal contact.

I have never seen such depravity stimulating such ecstasy.

Coney Island – it's the seduction of American maidenhood.

How many people have kissed for the first time in these twisting labyrinths and reached a conclusive decision on the question of marriage on their hour-long return journey by subway!

New York lovers must equate the happy life with just such an idiotic carnival.

On my way out, I decided that it was not the thing to leave Luna Park without even trying a single amusement. They were all the same to me, and I began a melancholy slinging of rings at the twirling figures of dolls.

I enquired beforehand about the price of this amusement. Eight rings cost twenty-five cents.

Having thrown sixteen rings, I nobly handed over a dollar, quite justifiably counting on receiving the half of it back.

The stallholder appropriated the dollar and asked me to show him what change I had. Not suspecting any skulduggery, I pulled out of my pocket about three dollars' worth of cents.

The ring-merchant shovelled the change from my palm

into his pocket and, upon my outraged exclamations, grabbed me by the sleeve, demanding the presentation of my banknotes. In amazement, I pulled out the ten dollars in my possession, which the grasping amusement-proprietor instantly pounced on. And only after entreaties from me and from my companions did he vouchsafe me the fifty cents for my return trip.

All in all, as the owner of this engaging game confirmed, I would have had to lob two hundred and forty-eight rings – that is to say, counting each go at just half a minute, more than two hours of solid work.

Arithmetic proved of no help at all, and my threat to contact the police was answered by a prolonged guffaw of good, healthy laughter.

A policeman, no doubt, would have arrogated to himself from this sum a good forty rings' worth.

It was later explained to me by Americans that this showman should have been given a good punch on the nose before he had the chance to demand as much as a second dollar.

Even if the money still then wasn't returned, you would nevertheless have earned respect as a real American – a 'good ole boy', or 'attaboy'!

Sunday life comes to an end at about two at night, and the whole of sober America – staggering buoyantly, or at least somewhat stimulated – goes back home.

ASPECTS OF NEW YORK LIFE ARE DIFFICULT. It is easy to utter any number of hackneyed phrases, completely unaccountable to anyone, about Americans – things like: the land of dollars, jackals of imperialism, and so on.

But this would only be one small frame in the enormous American film.

'Land of dollars' – this is something that every first-grade pupil knows. But if, by this, one has in mind the speculators' chase of the dollar that we had in 1919 during the fall of the rouble, or what they had in Germany in 1922 with the crash of the mark – when people with thousands, or millions, didn't buy bread rolls in the morning in the hope that they would be cheaper by the evening – then this would be a quite false conception.

Misers? No. A country that can eat a million dollars' worth a year, just of ice cream, can attract other labels to itself, rather than that one.

God is the dollar. The dollar is the Father. The dollar is the Holy Ghost.

But this isn't the penny-pinching meanness of people who just reconcile themselves to the necessity of having money, deciding to put by a pretty penny, so that they can later give up their profiteering, grow daisies in the garden, and put electric lights into the poultry houses of their precious broody hens. To this day New Yorkers delight in telling the 1911 story of cowboy Diamond Jim.[36]

Having come into an inheritance of two hundred and fifty thousand dollars, he hired an entire first-class train, stuffed it with wine and all his friends and relatives, and arrived in New York. Here he went off on a pub crawl round all the bars on Broadway, squandered a good half-million roubles' worth of dollars in two days, and then went back home to his mustangs on the filthy footboard of a goods train, without a cent to his name.

No! The attitude of the American to the dollar contains poetry. He knows that the dollar is the only power in his bourgeois country of a hundred and ten million (and in others, too). And I'm convinced that, all the attributes of money known to everyone apart, the American has an aesthetic admiration for the dollar's green back, associating it with spring, and the bull in the oval frame, seeming to him an image of the tough guy, a symbol of prosperity. And good old Lincoln on the dollar, and the possibility of every democrat fighting his way up towards emulating such people, renders the dollar the best and the most precious printed page that the younger generation can devour. On meeting you, an American will not greet you with a neutral – 'Good morning'.

He'll give you a friendly shout of – 'Make money?' – and then keep on walking.

An American will not use a vague phrase, like – 'You're looking bad (or good) today.'

An American will quantify it exactly:

'You're looking about two cents' worth today.' – Or:

'You look like a million dollars.'

It won't be said of you dreamily, so that the listener is lost in wonder: – 'He's a poet,' or an artist, or philosopher.

An American will quantify it exactly:

'This person is worth a million two hundred and thirty thousand dollars.'

With this, everything has been said: who your friends are, where you get invited, where you'll spend your summers, and so on.

The way by which you got your millions is of no concern in America. Everything is 'business'; and business matters are everything that makes a dollar. Getting royalties from poems that have sold out – that's business. If you can get away with stealing – then so is that.

Training for business begins from childhood. Well-off parents rejoice when their ten-year-old son, having thrown aside his books, manages to bring home the first dollar he has made from selling newspapers.

'He's going to be a real American!'

In the general ambience of business, inventiveness thrives.

In the children's camps – the summer boarding camps for

children, where they toughen their kids on swimming and football – it's forbidden to swear during boxing.

'How can you fight without swearing?' the distraught kids complained.

One of the budding businessmen took up this requirement.

A notice appeared on his tent:

'Five Russian swear words for a nickel. Fifteen for two nickels!'

Those desiring to study risk-free swearing, incomprehensible to their instructors, filled the whole tent.

The happy expert in Russian swearing, standing in the middle, conducted them all:

'All together, now: *durak*!'

'*Durak*!' (Bloody fool!)

'*Svoloch*'!' (Bloody swine!)

'Not *tvoloch*, but *svoloch*'!'

He had an uphill struggle with *sukin syn* (son of a bitch). The gormless American kids kept saying *zukin sin*', and the upright young businessman didn't want to palm them off with inferior swearing for good money.

Where adults are concerned, business takes on forms of epic grandeur.

Three years ago the candidate for some lucrative office in the city, a Mr Riegelmann, needed to be able to flaunt before the electorate some sort of public-spirited enterprise. He decided to construct a wooden boardwalk on the embankment for promenading along Coney Island.

The owners of the seaboard land-strip demanded a huge price – more than the position to come could have been worth. Riegelmann gave the owners a raspberry, repelled the ocean with sand and stone, created a strip of land three hundred and fifty feet wide, and lined the three and a half miles of shore with top-class boarding.

Riegelmann got elected.

Within a year, he had got back his losses with interest! In his capacity as an influential dignitary, he very profitably sold off all the display planks of his highly original enterprise for advertising purposes.

If even through oblique pressure of the dollar you can conquer office, fame and immortality, then, by immediately laying your money out, cash on the nail – you can buy anything.

Newspapers are launched by trusts. The trusts, and the bigwigs of the trusts, have sold themselves out to the advertisers, and the big store owners. Newspapers, as a whole, have so thoroughly sold out, and at such a high price, that the American press is considered incorruptible. There is no money that can bribe back an American journalist who has already sold out.

And if you are of such value that others will pay you more – then just prove it, and your boss will himself give you an increase.

A title? Certainly. Newspapers and theatrical warblers often ridicule the film star Gloria Swanson, a former maid who now makes fifteen thousand dollars a week, and her good-looking husband the count, with their Pacquin designs and their Anan shoes brought from Paris.

Love? Yes, indeed.

After the 'monkey trial',[37] the papers started sounding off about Mr Browning.

This millionaire, an agent for real estate sales, was seized in his old age with a youthful passion.

Given that marriage between an old man and a young girl was something disapproved of, the millionaire took the adoption road.

He advertised in the papers:

Millionaire Wishes to Adopt
Sixteen-Year-Old Girl

In response, twelve thousand flattering proposals with pictures of attractive girls poured in. At six in the morning, fourteen girls were already sitting in Mr Browning's reception room.

Browning adopted the very first one (such was his impatience), a Czech beauty named Maria Spas, who had let her hair down in childlike fashion. The next morning, the newspapers were panting away over Maria's good luck.

On the first day, sixty dresses were bought.

A pearl necklace was imported.

Over three days, these gift purchases amounted to more than forty thousand dollars.

And the daddy had himself photographed pawing his daughter's bosom, and with an expression on his face which would have been just perfect for a sly picture outside the brothels of Montmartre.

Fatherly happiness was disturbed by the news that this gentleman was trying, in passing, to adopt as well some thirteen-year-old girl from the following clutch of arrivals. The – albeit problematic – excuse could well have been that his 'daughter' had turned out to be a nineteen-year-old woman.

Three years younger here, three years older there. That's about equal – 'fifty-fifty', as the Americans say. All round, what does it matter?

In any event, the daddy justified himself not through this, but through the totality of his expenditure. He honourably demonstrated that the sum of his outgoings on this enterprise definitively showed that he was the only party to have come off worse.

The public attorney's office had to intervene. What happened after that, I don't know. The newspapers kept quiet, as though dollars had been stuffed in their mouths.

I am quite convinced that this same Browning would make serious corrective changes in the Soviet marriage code, bringing in restraints in the sphere of morality and probity.

There isn't a country that spits out as much moralistic, lofty, idealistic, sanctimonious rubbish as the United States does.

Compare this Browning, and his New York amusement, with a certain backwoods Texas scenario, where a gang of some forty old women, accusing a woman of prostitution and of sexual relations with their husbands, strip her naked, dip her in tar, shove her into feathers and fluff, and chase her out of town, through cackles of laughter, down the main streets.

Such are the medieval goings on, alongside the world's finest 'Twentieth Century' express train.

We can also nominate, as typical business and typical sanctimony, American sobriety – the dry law of 'prohibition'.

Whiskey is sold by everyone.

When you drop in to even the tiniest bar, you will see on all the tables a 'reserved' sign.

When an old hand comes into this same bar, he walks straight across, making for the opposite door.

The bar-owner blocks the way, throwing him a serious question:

'You are a gentleman?'

'Yes, I am,' rejoins the customer, presenting a green card. These are club members (there being thousands of clubs), or to put it simply – boozers who have been vouched for. The gentleman will be let through into the adjacent room. There several cocktail barmen with rolled-up sleeves are already hard at it, refreshing the content, colour and shape of their clients' glasses by the second at a very long counter.

Right here, at a couple of dozen tables, sit the diners. They gaze lovingly at a table, well stocked with every conceivable kind of beverage. After dinner, they put in their order:

'A shoebox!' – and out they go from the modest bar, hauling a new pair of whiskeys. And what tabs on this are the police keeping?

Tabs to ensure that they are not done out of their share.

The last wholesale 'bootlegger' to be caught had two hundred and forty policemen at his service.

The head of the struggle against alcohol bemoans his search for a dozen honest agents, threatening to give in his notice, since none such are to be found.

By now it is already impossible to repeal the law prohibiting the sale of alcohol, since this would disadvantage, first and foremost, the liquor merchants. And there is an army of such traders and intermediaries – one in five hundred of the population. Such a dollar base makes many of even the subtlest nuances of American life into a crude caricature of the proposition that consciousness and superstructure are determined by economics.

Should, in your presence, an ascetic[38] argument break out about feminine beauty, and those assembled divide into two camps – those in favour of bobhaired American women, and those preferring longhaired ones – then that still would not mean that you are surrounded by disinterested aesthetes.

No.

On the longhaired side, manufacturers of hairpins yell themselves hoarse – haircutting having undercut their production. Rooting for short hair is the hairdressers' union, since short hair on women has delivered up to hairdressers, from the human race, a whole second haircutting clientele.

If a lady will not walk down the street with you when you are carrying a pair of shoes from the cobbler's wrapped in newspaper, then you should realise that in the proliferation of attractive packaging the lead is being taken by the manufacturer of wrapping paper.

Even with regard to a relatively impartial thing, such as integrity, on which there's an entire literature, even in this regard, finance companies yell and agitate as they give loans to cashiers to cover the taking into pawn of pledges. For them it's important that cashiers deal honestly with other people's money, don't make off with the shop tills, and that the pledges rest in peace and don't vanish.

The same sort of dollar-financial considerations lie behind a somewhat idiosyncratic lively autumn game.

On 14th September, I was warned – 'Stop wearing your straw hat.'

On the 15th, on corners in front of hat shops, there stand gangs, dislodging straw hats, punching through the hard crowns of the hats, and, by the dozen, stringing these holed trophies down their arms.

In the autumn, it's indecent to go around in straw hats.

The observance of decency profits the purveyors of both soft and straw headgear. What would the soft-hat-makers do if straw hats were worn even in the winter? And what would become of the makers of the straw variety if people wore the same one year after year?

And the hat-punchers (head sometimes included) receive from the manufacturers a per-hat chewing gum allowance.

What I have just said about daily life in New York represents, of course, not the whole face of it. But still, it's some of the isolated features – the eyelashes, a freckle, one of the nostrils.

But these freckles and nostrils are extremely typical of a whole lower-middle-class mass, a mass that takes in almost the entire bourgeoisie – a mass catalysed by intermediate layers; a mass that has also swamped the better-provided-for section of the working class. That section is the one that has obtained a small house by mortgage payments, that pays for a small Ford car out of a weekly wage and, above all, is fearful of unemployment.

Unemployment – that would be a huge stride backwards: eviction from a house not paid off, repossession of the still not-quite-paid-for Ford, the end of a credit account at the butcher's, and so forth. And the workers of New York well remember the nights of the autumn of 1920 to 1921, when eighty thousand of the unemployed slept in Central Park.

The American bourgeoisie skilfully divides the workers by means of qualifications and earnings. One part constitutes the support for yellow leaders with three storeys of nape on their necks and cigars a yard and a half long, who are simply in hock to the bourgeoisie.

The other part, the revolutionary proletariat – that is to say the real one – does not get pulled into such prevailing financial dealings by jumped-up foremen. Such a proletariat both exists and fights. While I was there, the revolutionary couturiers from three locales (branches) of the Ladies' Garment Workers Union – locales two, nine and twenty-two – carried on a long struggle against their union's boss, chairman Morris Sigman, who was attempting to turn the union into a compliant subsection of the factory-owners' lackeys.[39] On the 20th of August, the United Committee for Action announced an anti-Sigman demonstration. About two thousand people demonstrated in Union Square and thirty thousand workers held a two-hour stoppage in solidarity. It was not purely coincidental that the demonstration was held in Union Square, opposite the windows of the Jewish Communist newspaper *Freiheit*.[40]

There was also a purely political demonstration, under the immediate organisation of the Communist party, apropos of the non-admission into America of the English Communist Member of Parliament, Saklatvala.[41]

New York has four Communist papers: *Novyi mir* ('New World', Russian), *Freiheit* ('Freedom', Jewish), *Shchodenni visti* ('Daily News', Ukrainian), and a Finnish one.

The *Daily Worker*, the central organ of the party, comes out in Chicago.

But these papers, representing a New York party membership of three thousand, in New York alone have a print run of sixty thousand.

It would be naive to overestimate the influence of Communist sympathisers of this magnitude, most of whom are foreign – it's pointless to expect imminent revolutionary activity in America. But it would also be foolish to underestimate this sixty thousand.

America

When anyone says 'America', the imagination will call to mind New York, American uncles, mustangs, Coolidge, and so on and so forth – trademarks of the North American United States.

This is strange, but true.

Strange – because there are as many as three Americas: North, Central and South.

The U.S.A. do not even take up the whole of the North – but never mind! – they have grabbed, appropriated and mixed up the name of all the Americas.

True, because the United States established the right to call itself 'America' by force, by means of dreadnoughts and dollars, putting fear into neighbouring republics and colonies.

Within the space of my short three-month stay alone, the Americans growled with their iron fist under the nose of the Mexicans, regarding a Mexican project for the nationalisation of their own inviolable subterranean depths. They sent detachments to the aid of some government being overthrown by the Venezuelan people. They gave unequivocal hints to England that, in the event of non-payment of debts, grain-producing Canada could be rattled. They wanted the same thing with regard to the French and just before the conference on repayment of French debt, they sent their pilots to Morocco on the French behalf, but then suddenly turned into Morocco-lovers and called back their pilots from humanitarian considerations.

Translated into plain Russian: send us your money, and you'll have the pilots.

Everybody knew that America and the United States of America were one and the same. Coolidge has only legalised this detail in one of his latest decrees – calling themselves, and only themselves, 'Americans'. The protesting roar from the dozens of republics, and even other United States comprising

America (the United States of Mexico, for example), was to no effect.

The word 'America' has now been definitively annexed.

But what lies concealed behind this word?

What is America, what sort of American nation is there, and what about the American spirit?

America I only saw from the windows of a train.

However, in relation to America, this shouldn't sound too bad, since all of it, length and breadth, is cross-cut by railway lines. They run in series – here four, there ten, then fifteen. And beyond these lines, at a jaunty angle, will be new tracks laid by new railway companies. There is no unified time-table, since the principal role of these lines is not to serve the interests of passengers, but those of the dollar and of adjacent industrialists.

Therefore, when you take a ticket at some station or other of a large city, you are never sure that this is the fastest, cheapest or most convenient means of communication between the towns you require. Especially as every single train is called an express, a courier train, or a fast train.

One train from Chicago to New York takes thirty-two hours, another one takes twenty-four, and a third one takes twenty. They are all called the same thing – express.

On the expresses, people sit with their train ticket shoved into their hatbands. It's more relaxing that way. You don't have to worry about looking for your ticket, and the conductor slides an experienced hand behind your hatband and is quite astonished if there isn't a ticket there. If you are travelling in a sleeping car, the celebrated Pullman, considered in America the most comfortable and snug way, then your entire organisational system will be convulsed twice daily, morning and evening, by a senseless, idiotic kerfuffle. At nine in the evening they start to wreck the daytime carriage, lowering the beds that are folded up to the ceiling; they turn down the bedding, attach iron rods, thread up the curtain rings, and clatter into place the iron partitions. All of these intricate contrivances spring into action, so as to rig up, along the sides of the carriage in two tiers, twenty curtained-off sleeping berths, leaving down the middle a narrow – not so much gangway, as a scant crawlway.

In order to crawl through at bed-making time, you have to manoeuvre repeatedly past the backsides of two Negro attendants, whose heads have vanished into the beds they are making.

You turn and lead one of them almost outside the carriage – for two people can scarcely get past each other, especially with the ladder for climbing up to the top tier – then you swap places and worm your way back down the carriage. Getting undressed, you frenziedly try to hold closed the ever-opening curtains, in order to avert outraged exclamations from the disrobing sixty-year-old females opposite, who run some society for Christian girls.

While this work is going on, you forget to squeeze in tight your bare feet, which are sticking out from under the curtain – and a cursed great hefty Negro tramples on your corns. From nine in the morning, there begins the bacchanalia of the stripping of the sleeping cars and restoring the carriage to its 'sitting condition'.

Our European division into compartments, even of the 'hard' seated carriages, is far more practical than this American 'Pullman' system.

What really surprised me is the way that trains in America can be late, even without any special reason or mishap.

I had to travel urgently overnight from giving a lecture in Chicago to a lecture in Philadelphia – an express journey of twenty hours. But at that time of night there was only one train route operating, with two changes. The ticket clerk, despite the five minutes connection time allowed, could not and would not guarantee arrival in time for my connection, although he did add that the chances of being late were slight. It's possible that the non-committal answer is explicable by an inclination to disparage the rival lines.

At the train stops, passengers leap out, buy up bunches of celery, and jump back on, chewing at the stalks on the run.

There is iron in celery. Iron is good for Americans. Americans love celery.

As we go, uncleared woods of the Russian variety flash past, football pitches with varicoloured players – and technology, technology and technology.

This technology is not static; this technology is growing. It does have one strange feature – from the outside: outwardly, this technology produces a not quite finished, temporary impression.

It's as if the construction, the walls of a factory, were not really sound – a thing of a day, a thing for a year.

The telegraph posts, and quite often the tramway columns even, are nearly always wooden.

The huge gas-holders, a match thrown into which would blow away half the city, seem to be unguarded. Only in wartime was there a guard placed there.

Why should this be?

It occurs to me that it stems from the acquisitive, aggressive nature of American development.

Technical development is broader here than the all-embracing Germanic variety, but it doesn't have within it an older technological tradition, which would impel not only the piling up of buildings, but the layout of railings and a quadrangle in front of a factory, to blend in with the structural design as a whole.

We were driving from Beacon (six hours' drive away from New York) and ended up without any warning bang in the middle of total roadworks, with no space left whatever for cars. (The local owners were obviously having it laid for their own benefit and were not too bothered about through passage.) We turned into the side roads and found a way out only by quizzing people we happened to meet, there being no signs at all to indicate directions.

In Germany this would be unthinkable under any circumstances, even in the back of beyond.

For all the grandiose qualities of America's building, and although the American construction rate, the height of American skyscrapers, their facilities and spaciousness are unattainable for Europe – even America's houses generally give off a strangely provisional impression.

Or perhaps it just seems like that.

It seems like that because, on the top of a huge building, there stands a capacious water tank. Water is supplied up to the sixth floor by the city, and beyond that the building itself takes responsibility. Even if one wants to believe in the omnipotence of American technology, such a building looks contrived, hastily converted from whatever it might have been, and due for demolition upon the rapid completion of its moment of indispensability.

This characteristic stands out as completely repellent in constructions appearing in the first place to be essentially temporary.

I was at Rockaway Beach (a sort of seaside satellite for New Yorkers of average means). I haven't seen anything more repulsive than the buildings stuck on to the shore there. I couldn't live even for two hours in that kind of a Karelian cigarette case.

All the standardised houses are identical, like matchboxes of the one make and the one shape. The houses are transfixed, like tram passengers in the springtime, returning from (Moscow's) Sokolniky Park on a Sunday evening. Opening the bathroom window, you can see everything that's happening in the neighbours' bathroom, and if the neighbours' door is half open, then you can see right through the house to the next holidaymakers' bathroom. These homes stand erect along a narrow belt of alleys, like soldiers on parade – ear to ear. The structural materials are such that you can hear not only every whisper and sigh of your neighbour in love, but through the walls you can discern the subtlest nuances of the aromas from next door's dining table.

That kind of a resort village is the absolute ideal as a set-up for small-mindedness and scandal – on a worldwide scale.

Even the big, latest and most luxurious housing blocks seem temporary, because all America, and New York in particular, is under construction, under interminable construction. Ten-storey buildings are pulled apart to build twenty-storey ones; twenty-storey ones for thirty-storey ones – for forty, and so on.

New York is perpetually filled with heaps of stones and steel transoms, the screeching of drills and the pounding of hammers.

Real and powerful construction fever!

Americans do their building as though they were acting through for the thousandth time the most fascinating and closely studied of plays. Tearing oneself away from this spectacle of know-how and gumption is all but impossible.

A mechanical digger is placed on a piece of bare ground. With the appropriate clanking, it gnaws and sucks up soil and, on the spot, spits it out into the continuously passing trucks. In the middle of the construction site, up goes the crane for hoisting girders. It picks up huge steel pipes and bangs them into the hard ground with a steam hammer (one that snuffles, as though all technology were catarrhal), as if they were mere paper tacks. Workers only guide the hammer onto the pipe and check the surfaces with a spirit level. Other paws of the crane lift steel props and cross-beams, which slot into place completely smoothly – they just need knocking and screwing together!

The building goes up, and the crane goes up with it, as though they were lifting the house from the ground by the hair. Within a month, if not sooner, they'll remove the crane – and the building is ready.

This is a version for building of the golden rule for the manufacture of cannons (find a hole, surround it with cast iron, and you've got your cannon). They took a cubic quantity of air, screwed some steel round it – and the building is ready. It's difficult to relate seriously to this. So you react with a sort of poetic inspiration to some twenty-storey Cleveland hotel or other, of which the locals say: 'Hey, that building is crowding us' (just like being in a tram – 'move down a bit, please!') – and so they're just relocating it, ten blocks away, to the lake.

I don't know precisely who will be relocating this building, or how, but if a thing like that slips from their hands, it will trample a lot of corns.

Over ten years or so, building in concrete puts a completely different face on the big cities.

Thirty years ago, V.G. Korolenko, on seeing New York, noted: 'Through the shoreline haze, there appeared huge buildings of six and seven storeys.'[42]

About fifteen years ago, Maxim Gorky, having visited New York, apprised us: 'Through the driving rain, along the shore could be seen buildings of fifteen and twenty storeys.'[43]

So as not to deviate too far from the paths of decorum trodden by these writers, I ought to expatiate as follows: 'Through the driving smoke, one can see some quite reasonable buildings of forty and fifty storeys.'

Whereas a budding poet, after such an expedition, might record: 'Through the upright buildings of an indeterminate number of storeys erected on the New York shoreline, were to be seen no smoke, no driving rains, and furthermore no haze whatsoever.'

The American nation.

Of it, more than of any other, may be said, in the words of one of the first revolutionary posters: 'You get various Americans: those who are proletarians, and those who are bourgeois'.

The offspring of Chicago millionaires kill children (the Loeb and company case) out of curiosity; the court finds them to be abnormal and spares their precious lives.[44] The 'abnormals' live on, running prison libraries, captivating their fellow prisoners with sophisticated philosophical compositions.

Defenders of the working class (the case of Vanzetti and the other comrades) get condemned to death – and entire committees, organised to save them, so far are not strong enough to force the state governor to revoke the sentence.[45] The bourgeoisie is armed and organised. The Ku Klux Klan has become a commonplace.

The clothing workers of New York, over the days of the Klan's costumed convention, advertised to attract orders for tall hats and white robes, announcing:

'Welcome, Ku Klux Klan!'

In the cities there is sometimes news that some Klan leader or other has killed someone or other, and hasn't yet been caught. Another (lacking a surname) has raped a third girl and thrown her from his car – and is also going around town without a handcuff in sight. Alongside the aggressive Klan organisations, you find the peaceable Masonic ones. A hundred thousand Masons in variegated eastern costume wander the streets of Philadelphia the day before their festival.

This army has retained its lodges and its hierarchy, and makes itself understood, as of old, by secret gestures, the gesticulation of one of the fingers by a waistcoat button tracing mysterious signs on meeting. But in reality, in the main, it has long since become an exclusive sort of distribution enterprise of the major traders and manufacturers, who nominate dignitaries and the country's most important functionaries. It must seem preposterous to observe this medieval hangover in procession along the Philadelphia streets beneath the windows of the *Philadelphia Enquirer* printing-works, which throws out four hundred and fifty thousand copies an hour from its rotary presses.

Alongside this close-knit fraternity is the odd existence of the legalised – obviously, just to be on the safe side, and facilitate observation – Workers' Communist Party of America, and the more than odd existence of those daring to engage in the struggle for professional unions.

I saw, on my first day in Chicago, in the cold and the pouring rain, the following unbridled scene.

Around a huge factory building, there wove a ceaseless procession of soaking, thin, benumbed people; from the roadways, great fat mackintoshed policemen were keenly watching.

The factory was on strike. The workers have to chase off the strike-breakers and caution any hired on false premises.

But they do not have the right to stop – the police will arrest anyone stationary on the grounds of laws against picketing. You can speak to people on the move, hit out as you walk. It's a weird sort of ten-hour vigorous working day.

No less prickly are the national interrelationships in America. I have already written about the masses of foreigners in America (of course, the whole place is an amalgamation of foreigners for the purposes of exploitation, speculation and commerce). They live here for decades without any loss of language or customs.

In Jewish New York at New Year, exactly like Shavli, you will see young men and women dressed up, as though either for a wedding or for a coloured photograph. The women are in patent-leather shoes, orange stockings, a white lace dress, a multicoloured kerchief and a Spanish comb in their hair. The men are in the same kind of shoes and some kind of cross between a frock coat, a jacket and a tuxedo. And across their bellies they have a chain of either real or American gold – the size and weight of the chains that keep the back door closed to robbers. Those helping at the service are in striped shawls. The children have hundreds of congratulatory cards covered with hearts and doves – cards which weigh down all the New York postmen expectantly over these days, and which constitute the only item in universal demand in all the department stores throughout the run-up to the holiday.

In another area, Russians live just as exclusively, and Americans visit the antique shops of that quarter, to buy an exotic samovar.

The language of America is the imaginary language of the pandemonium of Babel, with just the one difference – that there the languages were mixed so that no one understood them, whereas here they are mixed so that everyone understands them. The result is that from, let's say English, you get a language comprehensible to all nationalities – except for the English.

It's for good reason, so they say, that in Chinese shops you find the notice:

HERE ENGLISH IS SPOKEN
AND AMERICAN IS UNDERSTOOD

For me, not knowing the English language, it's still easier to understand a tight-lipped American than a manically garrulous Russian.

A Russian will use English loan words like 'streetcar', 'corner', 'block', 'boarder' and 'ticket', and will say things like: 'You will journey without the exchanges of stoppings.'

That means that you have a straight-through ticket.

The expression 'an American', brings to mind, for us in Russia, a cross between O. Henry's eccentric hoboes, Nick Carter and his inevitable pipe, and the chequered cowboys of the Kuleshov film studio.[46]

There ain't no such thing.

It's the white man who calls himself 'an American'. He considers even the Jew to be black, and will not shake hands with the Negro. If he sees a Negro with a white woman, he'll chase the Negro home with a revolver. He himself will rape black girls with impunity, and will subject a black man who goes anywhere near a white woman to lynch law – that is to say, he'll tear off his arms and legs and roast him alive over a bonfire. It's a custom even more extreme than our 'business of the burning of the gypsy horse-thieves in Listviany village'.[47]

Why should these people be considered 'Americans' and not, for example, the Negroes?

The Negroes, from whom comes what is called American dance – the foxtrot, the shimmy and American jazz! The Negroes, who bring out a lot of fine magazines – *Opportunity*, for example.[48] The Negroes, who are endeavouring to find their links with world culture – and do find them, when we consider Pushkin, Alexandre Dumas, the artist Henry Tan and others as artisans of their culture.[49]

Only just recently, the Negro publisher Caspar Holstein announced a prize of a hundred dollars, in the name of the greatest Negro poet, A.S. Pushkin, for the best Negro poem.

This prize will be awarded on 1st May 1926.

And why shouldn't the Negroes consider Pushkin their writer? Why, even now Pushkin wouldn't be allowed into a single 'respectable' hotel or salon in New York. Well, Pushkin did have curly hair and a Negroid blueness under his nails.

When the so-called scales of history begin to tilt, much will depend with regard to which pan the twelve million Negroes decide to pile their twenty-four million weighty hands onto. The Negroes who are heated up over the bonfires of Texas may yet prove to be a sufficiently dry powder for explosions of revolution.

Spirit, and that includes American spirit, is an incorporeal thing – scarcely even a thing at all. It doesn't have an office, it doesn't exactly export strongly, it takes up nothing in the way of tonnage – and if it drains anything itself, then it's only whiskey, and even then it won't be American, it'll be imported.

And so not very much interest is taken in spirit; and the little that is taken has surfaced only recently, when the bourgeoisie, after a period of out-and-out banditry and exploitation, has taken on a certain air of calm and assured benevolence. There's now a certain fatty layer of bourgeois poets, thinkers and artists.

Americans envy the European styles. They understand perfectly well that, for their money, they could have not just fourteen but even twenty-eight Louis. But their haste, and their propensity for the punctual completion of what has been projected, leave them neither the inclination nor the time to wait for today's structures to settle into an American style. Therefore Americans buy up European art – both the *objets d'art* and the artists. They preposterously decorate their fortieth storeys with some Renaissance piece or other, oblivious to the fact that these statuettes and curlicues are good enough at six storeys, but any higher they are completely unnoticeable. Of course, these high-class baubles can't be placed any lower, or they would interfere with advertisements, placards and other such essential things.

There is one building beside the public library that strikes me as the epitome of stylistic monstrosity. It's all smooth, economical, shapely and black, but with a pointed roof, painted gold for added glamour.

In 1912, some Odessan poets, as a publicity stunt, gilded the nose of the cashier who was selling the tickets for their poetry reading.

A rather delayed and inflated instance of plagiarism.

The streets of New York are decorated with small mementoes of writers and artists from the whole world over. The walls of the Carnegie Institute are inscribed with the names of Tchaikovsky, Tolstoy and others.

More recently, the voices of young workers from the sphere of art are being raised in protest against half-baked, eclectic banality.

Americans are trying to find a soul – the rhythm of America. They are starting to deduce an American walk from the tentative steps of the ancient Indians on the footpaths of an empty Manhattan. Surviving Indian families are painstakingly conserved, like museum pieces. Remote kinship with any of the well-known Indian tribes is considered the height of fashion in high society – something which, even quite recently, was regarded as a thundering disgrace in American eyes. Artistic figures not born in America are simply ceasing to be listened to.

All sorts of localisms are beginning to become all the rage.

CHICAGO. In 1920, in my fanciful narrative poem *150,000,000*, I depicted Chicago as follows:[50]

> *The world,*
> *from fragments of light*
> *gathering a quintet,*
> *endowed [America] with a power that's magical –*
> *a city therein stands*
> *on a single spiral –*
> *it's all electro-dynamo-mechanical.*

In Chicago
there are 14,000 streets –
beams of suns of the squares.
From each –
go 700 side streets,
in length a year for a train.
It's fantastic for a person in Chicago![51]

The most famous present-day American poet, Carl Sandburg, who is himself from Chicago, and was driven by the American unwillingness to grapple with lyric poetry into the 'News Items and Events' section of the richest newspaper, the *Chicago Tribune* – this is how this same Sandburg[52] describes Chicago:

Chicago

HOG Butcher for the World,
Tool Maker, Stacker of Wheat,
Player with Railroads and the Nation's Freight Handler;
Stormy, husky, brawling,
City of the Big Shoulders.

  ...

And they tell me you are crooked and I answer: Yes, it is
 true I have seen the gunman kill and go free to kill again.
And they tell me you are brutal and my reply is: On the
 faces of women and children I have seen the marks of
 wanton hunger.

  ...

Flinging magnetic curses amid the toil of piling job on job,
 here is a tall bold slugger set vivid against the little soft
 cities;

...
Bareheaded,
Shovelling,
Wrecking,
Planning,
Building, breaking, rebuilding,
...
Laughing the stormy, husky, brawling laughter of Youth,
half naked, sweating, proud to be Hog Butcher, Tool
Maker, Stacker of Wheat, Player with Railroads and
Freight Handler to the Nation.

The guidebooks and the old stagers say:

Chicago:
The biggest abattoirs.
The biggest procurer of timber materials.
The biggest furniture centre.
The biggest producer of agricultural machinery.
The biggest piano depot.
The biggest manufacturer of iron stoves.
The most important railway centre.
The biggest centre for mail order distribution.
The most thickly populated corner of the world.
The most utilised bridge on earth: Bush Street Bridge.
The best boulevard system in the entire world – walk
along the boulevards, and walk right round Chicago,
without having to set foot on any mere street.

Everything is the biggest, the most, the most...

What sort of a city is Chicago?

If all American cities were to be poured into a bag, and all the buildings shaken up like lotto numbers, then even the city mayors themselves would not be able to pick out their own domains.

But there is Chicago, and this Chicago differs from all the other cities – differs not by its buildings, not by its people, but by its particular Chicago style of unflinching energy.

In New York, many things are for decoration, for show.

The Great White Way is for show, Coney Island is for show – even the fifty-seven-storey Woolworth Building is for rubbing it in, to the provincials and the foreigners.

Chicago can live without bluster.

The ostentatious skyscraper part is narrow, and tucked in against the shore by an immense manufacturing Chicago.

Chicago is not ashamed of its factories; it doesn't relegate them to the outskirts. There can be no surviving without bread, and McCormick puts his agricultural machinery plants on display more centrally, even more haughtily, than any Paris can do its Notre-Dame.

There can be no surviving without meat, and there's nothing to be said for dalliance with vegetarianism – and therefore at the very centre you find the bleeding heart, the abattoirs.

The Chicago abattoirs are one of the vilest sights I have ever seen. You drive straight in, in a Ford, onto an extremely long wooden bridge. This bridge stretches above thousands of pens for bulls, calves and sheep, and for an innumerable quantity of the world's pigs. A squealing, mooing and bleating overpowers this place – the like of which will not be heard again until the end of the world, when people and livestock get squashed between merging rock faces. Through your tightly clenched nostrils seeps the sour stench of bulls' urine, and ten types of cattle crap in a measure of millions.

The imaginary – or the real – smell of an entire sea of spilt blood sends your head spinning.

Flies, in a variety of sort and calibre, flitter across from puddles and liquid filth, now onto the eyes of cows, and now onto your eyes.

Long wooden corridors carry off the recalcitrant livestock.

If the rams will not go of their own accord, a trained goat will lead them.

Where the corridors end is where the knives of the pig- and bull-slaughterers begin.

A machine hoists the live squealing pigs by a hook, having caught them by a living leg, throws them on to a conveyor belt, and they drift legs upward past an Irishman or a Negro who sticks his knife into the porcine throat. Each man knifes several thousand pigs a day, boasted our abattoir escort.

Here you get all the squealing and the snorting, but at the other end of the works they are already putting seals on the legs of meat – while tin cans, discharged like hailstones, flash in the sun like streaks of lightning. Further on refrigerators are being loaded and ham whizzes by express train and steamboat to the meat-merchants and restaurants of the entire world.

We are driving for about fifteen minutes along the bridge of just one company.

And from all sides, dozens of companies yell at you with their signs.

Wilson!

Star!

Swift!

Hammond!

Armour!

And by the way, all these companies, the law notwithstanding, form one conglomerate, a single trust. At the head of this trust is Armour – and the power of the whole enterprise can be judged by its reach.

Armour has over a hundred thousand workers. Armour has ten to fifteen thousand employees in its offices alone.

Four hundred million dollars is the total value of the Armour resources. Eighty thousand shareholders have acquired shares, and they are now trembling over the reliability of the Armour enterprise and picking off any specks of dust they can from the directors.

Half the shareholders are workers (half, of course, of the number of shareholders, not of shares). They give the workers shares on payment by instalments – one dollar a week. Through these shares, the temporary compliance of a backward abattoir workforce is assured.

Armour is proud.

Sixty per cent of American meat production, and ten per cent worldwide, is supplied just by Armour.

Armour's canned products are eaten by the world.

Anyone can get gastritis.

Even during the World War there were tinned foods on the front lines with modified relabelling. In the hunt for fresh profits, Armour was getting rid of four-year-old eggs and tinned meat as old as the call-up age – twenty years old!

The more naive, wanting to have a look at the capital of the United States, travel to Washington. More urbane people go to a tiny little street in New York – Wall Street, the banking street, the street that in effect governs the country.

This is nearer the truth, and it's cheaper than a trip to Washington. Here, and not in Coolidge's town, is where the foreign powers ought to be maintaining their ambassadors. There is a subway tunnel under Wall Street – and if it were to be stuffed with dynamite and detonated, then this whole little street would be blown to merry hell!

Flying into the air would go: all the investment ledgers, the titles and successions of innumerable stocks and shares, and vast rolls of foreign debts.

Wall Street is first of the capitals, the capital of the American dollar. Chicago is the second capital, the capital of industry.

Therefore it wouldn't be so incorrect to put Chicago in place of Washington. Pig-slaughtering Wilson has no less an influence on American life than had Woodrow of that ilk.

The abattoirs do not endure without trace. Having worked there for a bit, you will either turn vegetarian, or you will start quietly killing people – once you've had your fill of cinema. It's not by pure chance that Chicago is the location for sensational killings and the legendary home of the big criminals.

It's not by chance that in this air one in every four babies dies before they are a year old.

It is understandable that the magnitude of the army of toilers, and the dismal quality of Chicago working life, should, indeed here, arouse the labouring masses to the greatest opposition encountered in America.

Here is to be found the main strength of the Workers' Party of America.

Here – is the central committee.

Here – too is its central newspaper – the *Daily Worker*.

Here is where the party turns with its appeals, when it needs to generate thousands of dollars from meagre wages.

It's with the voice of the Chicagoans that the party roars when it needs to remind the Secretary of State, Mr Kellogg, that allowing only servants of the dollar into the United States is not good enough; that America is not the house of Kellogg; and that, sooner or later, he'll have to let in as well the Communist Saklatvala and other representatives of the world's working class.

It wasn't today, and it wasn't yesterday either, that the workers of Chicago started out on the revolutionary road.

Just as, in Paris, visiting Communists go to the bullet-ridden wall of the Commune, so they go in Chicago to the monument to the first hanged revolutionaries.

On 1st May 1886 the Chicago workers announced a general strike. On 3rd May there was a demonstration at the McCormick works, in the course of which the police provoked some shots. These shots presented justification for police shooting and gave cause for the seizure of the ringleaders.

Five comrades – August Spies, Adolph Fischer, Albert Parsons, Louis Lingg and George Engel – were hanged.[53]

Now, on the stone commemorating their common grave, may be read words from the speech made by one of the accused:

'The day will come when our silence will be more powerful than the voices you are throttling today.'

Chicago does not rub your nose in technological high style. But even the superficial appearance of the city, even its outward life, shows that, more than other cities, Chicago lives by what it produces, lives by its machinery.

Here, at every stage, a lift-bridge can rise in front of your car radiator, allowing steamboats and barges through to Lake Michigan. Here, when you're driving over a bridge suspended above the railway lines, at any hour of the morning, you will be engulfed in the smoke and the steam of hundreds of rushing steam engines.

Here, at every turn of your steering wheel, the filling stations owned by the kings of petroleum – Standard Oil and Sinclair – flash past.

Here the automatic warning lights at the crossings blink through the night, as do the sunken fluorescent lamps, marking off the pavements to avoid accidents. Here the special mounted police note down the registration numbers of any cars standing in front of a building for more than half an hour. If everyone were allowed to stay parked on the streets for as long as they liked, cars would be standing in rows ten deep and piled ten layers high.

This is why a Chicago all in gardens should be depicted on a single spiral and as utterly electro-dynamo-mechanical. I say this not in defence of my own poem, but an assertion of the poet's right and obligation to organise and rework visible material and not just to polish up the visible.

The guidebook's description of Chicago is correct, but it's nothing like it.

Sandburg's description is both incorrect and nothing like it.

My description is incorrect, but it's something like it.

Critics wrote that my Chicago could only have been concocted by someone who had never seen this city.

They said that, were I to see Chicago, I would alter my description.

Now I have seen Chicago. I tested the poem on citizens of Chicago. It didn't provoke sceptical smiles from them; on the contrary, it would appear to have shown them another side to Chicago.

DETROIT is the second and last of the American cities on which I shall be expanding.[54] Unfortunately, I did not manage to see the prairie grain areas. The American railways are way too expensive. A Pullman to Chicago costs fifty dollars (a hundred roubles).

I was only able to travel to where there are large Russian, and of course working-class, colonies. My readings were organised by *Novyi mir* and *Freiheit*, the Russian and Jewish newspapers of the Workers' Party of America.

In Detroit there are twenty thousand Russians.

In Detroit there are eighty thousand Jews.

In the main, these are former paupers – Russians who speak only dreadful ill of Russia, having arrived here about twenty years ago, and are therefore well, or at least tolerably, disposed towards the Soviet Union. The exception is a group of Wrangelites,[55] brought over from Constantinople by grey-headed and bald-headed warrior leaders of the Union of Christian

Youth, but this lot too will soon get absorbed. The dollar is better than any agitation at making the White emigration crumble. The celebrated Kirilitsa,[56] whom the Americans called 'Princess Cyril', who turned up in America looking for Washington's recognition, soon gave up. She found herself a smart entrepreneur-manager and started stretching out her hand for kissing at ten to fifteen dollars a go in the Monday Morning opera club in New York.

Even 'Prince' Boris[57] plunged straight into New York with no holds barred.

Taking a leaf out of Rodchenko's[58] book, he started to go in for real photomontage, wrote pieces on earlier court life, and enumerated precisely when and with whom the tsars had got drunk, illustrating his *feuilletons* with montages of ballerinas on tsars' laps. He reminisced about his card games with tsars – while he was at it, sticking montages of former tsars onto casino scenes the world over. Even the most inveterate of White Guards were crestfallen at these Borisian œuvres. How can you ever propagandise for a White Guard restoration through characters like that? Even the White newspapers recorded with sadness that such carryings-on left the very idea of monarchism utterly phlegm-besmirched. Newly brought over and still unenlightened White Guards nose around the companies here; many have been taken under the wing of Ford – who is graciously disposed to any shade of whiteness.

The Ford workers show such people to their Russian novices: 'Look, your tsar is working here.' But this tsar doesn't do much – for at Ford's there's a kind of tacit rule that White Russians should be instantly welcomed and not troubled with much work.

In Detroit there are many huge global enterprises – for example, Parke-Davis medicaments. But the glory of Detroit is its automobiles.

I'm not sure how many people there are here to one motor car (I think it may be four to one), but I know that on the streets there are many more cars than there are people.

People call in to shops, offices, cafés and diners – and their motors await them by the doors. They stand parked in continuous rows along both sides of the street. They bunch together in rallies in special fenced-off spaces, where cars can be parked for twenty-five to thirty-five cents.

In the evening, anyone wishing to park a car has to drive from a main street onto a side street, and then drive up and down for about ten minutes. After parking in an enclosed area, he will later on have to wait for it to be extricated from somewhere in the middle of thousands of other cars.

And since a motor car is larger than a human being, and a person going out also gets into a motor car, then the abiding impression is created that there are more cars than people.

Here you find the factories of:

Packard.

Cadillac.

Dodge Brothers: the world's second largest – they do fifteen hundred cars a day.

But, over all these, towers the name – Ford.

Ford have really established themselves here, and seven thousand brand new Fords trundle out daily from the gates of their non-stop night-and-day factory.

At one end of Detroit is Highland Park, with blocks of buildings for forty-five thousand workers; at the other end is River Rouge, with sixty thousand. And, what's more, in Dearborn, seventeen miles from Detroit, there's an aircraft assembly works.

I visited the Ford factory in a state of great excitement. Ford's book published in Leningrad in 1923 had '45,000 copies' stamped on it. 'Fordism' is the most popular term among our labour organisers. They talk about the Ford enterprise almost as though it were an entity that could be transposed, without any changes, to the socialist system.

Professor Lavrov, in his preface to the fifth edition of Ford's book, writes: 'This book by Ford has appeared... the matchless car model... those who come after Ford are to be pitied, the reason for this lying in the ingenuity of the system devised by Ford, which, like any perfect system, cannot but guarantee the most efficient organisation...' – and so on, and so forth.[59]

Ford himself says that the goal of his theory is to make the world into a source of happiness (the socialist!). If we don't learn better to exploit machines, then we won't have enough time left to enjoy the trees and the birds, the flowers and the meadows. 'Money is useful only in so far as it provides the means for freedom in life' (the capitalist?). 'If you work for the sake of work itself, for the satisfaction which comes from knowing that you are doing something right, then money will generate itself aplenty' (not something I had noticed!). 'The boss (Ford) is a companion to his employee, and the worker is a friend to his boss.' 'We don't want excessive labour that would wear people out. Each Ford worker should, and could, think up improvements to the procedure – and then he too could be a candidate to become a Ford', and so on, and so forth.

I deliberately do not linger any further on the valuable and interesting thoughts in that book. There has been enough trumpeting of these, and it's not really for them that the book was written.

As for factory tours, people are ushered along in groups of fifty. There is just one route through the works, laid down once and for all. In front goes a Ford man. The visitors go in single file, with no stopping.

To get permission, you fill in a form in a room, which is the one where the ten millionth celebratory Ford is standing, covered all over with inscriptions. You get your pockets stuffed with Ford advertising, piles of which are lying all over the tables. The form-pushers and the guides have about them the air of aged, superannuated sales-barkers from cut-price stalls.

Off we go! The floors have been licked clean. No one can stop, not for a second. People in hats walk about, watching and continually making notes on sheets of paper. Evidently, this is the recording of working practices. You hear neither voices, nor isolated reverberations. There's just a universal, serious hum. The faces have a greenish tinge, with black lips, like at a film shoot. This comes from the daylight-like strip lighting. Beyond the tool shop, beyond the metal-punching and casting rooms – this is where the famous Ford assembly line begins. Work moves along in front of the worker. Naked chassis perch there, as though the cars have not yet got their trousers on. They put on the mudguards, and the car moves along with you towards the engine fitters. Cranes fix on the bodies; wheels roll into place; tyres trundle down non-stop from beneath the ceiling, like bread rolls; and workers hammer something into place from under the assembly line. Workers are stuck to the sides on little, low trolleys. After passing through thousands of hands, the car acquires its look at one of the final stages. A driver gets into the vehicle. The car drives off the assembly line and coasts out into the compound under its own power.

This is a process already familiar from the newsreels, but, all the same, you come out from it completely stunned.

We still have to go through some accessory departments (Ford's themselves make all the parts for their cars, from the thread to the glass), where there are bales of wool, and thousands of kilos of crankshafts flying over your head on hoisted circuits. We go past the Ford power station, the world's mightiest, and come out onto Woodward Street.

My companion on this tour, an old Ford employee who gave up the job within two years because of tuberculosis, was also seeing the whole plant for the first time. He said, with some fury: 'They're just showing us the classy side – I'd have taken you to the River forges, where half of them work in an inferno, and the other half in filth and water.'

That evening, some Ford employees – working correspondents on the Chicago Communist *Daily Worker* – were telling me:

'It's bad. Really bad. There are no spittoons. Ford doesn't provide any. He says: "I don't need you to be spitting, what I need is for it to be clean – and if you really have to spit, you can buy the spittoons yourselves."'

'Technological advance – technology's for him, not for us.'

'He gives you goggles with thick glass, so you don't put your eyes out. The glass is costly. Seems humanitarian. The reason he does this is that, with thin glass, the eyepieces would get broken and this would cost money. But with thick glass you only get scratches remaining; they ruin your eyes in a couple of years anyway, but he doesn't have to pay for that.'

'For a meal break, it's fifteen minutes. You eat at your workbench, without anything to drink. He needs to look at the labour regulations about obligatory separate eating space.'

'There is no paid time off, whatsoever.'

'And trade union members are just not taken on at all. There's no library. There's just a cinema – and even that only shows films about faster working methods.'

'And do you think we don't get any accidents here? Well, we do. But they never get reported, and those injured and killed get carted away in an ordinary Ford, and not in any red-crossed vehicle.'

'His work system purports to be an hourly one (the eight-hour working day), but in fact it's sheer piecework.'

'But how can you fight Ford?'

'Spooks, provocateurs, fraternities – it's eighty per cent foreigners everywhere here.'

'How do you conduct agitation in fifty-four languages?'

At four o'clock, I stood by the Ford gates, watching the outgoing shift. Workers staggered onto the trams and, completely done in, fell asleep straight away.

In Detroit, you find the highest divorce rate. The Ford system gives its workers impotence.

Departure

The Transatlantic Company's quayside is at the bottom of Fourteenth Street.

The suitcases were put onto a continually rising conveyor belt equipped with slats, so that things don't slip back. The things zipped up to the second floor.

Against the quayside a small steamship had docked, the *Rochambeau*, which had then become even smaller in juxtaposition to the huge quay, like a two-storey riding school.

Steps descended disdainfully from the upper floor.

Having inspected them first, they take away your exit documents – evidence that American taxes on any earnings here have been paid, and that the person concerned had entered the country properly, with authorised permission.

They checked my ticket – and now I'm on French territory. I am not allowed back under the French Line sign, or under the advertisement for the National Biscuit Company.

I have a good look at the passengers for the last time. For the last time – because autumn is the season for storms, and people will be lying flat out for the whole eight days.

On arrival at Le Havre, I found out that, on the liner leaving at the same time as we did from the Cunard Line quay, six people smashed in their noses by falling against washbasins during the lurching that sent waves rolling across all the decks.

The boat's not much of a thing. It's in a class of its own: it only has first and third class. There's no second. Or, to be more exact, there's nothing but second. Those who travel on it are either hard up or thrifty, along with a few young Americans, neither thrifty nor hard up, who are being dispatched by their parents to study the arts in Paris.

New York, so impressive on arrival, sailed away, waving its handkerchiefs.

The Metropolitan Building, translucent with its windows, turned its forty storeys away. The new telephone building broke up like a pile of cubes. The whole nest of skyscrapers had moved back and, at a distance, all at once became visible. There was the Benenson Building, about forty-five storeys high; two indistinguishable corset boxes, the names of which I don't know; streets, rows of raised railway, and subway tunnels ending at the Sutton Ferry wharf. Then the buildings melted into a craggy, precipitous rock face, above which the fifty-seven-storey Woolworth Building towered like a funnel.

The American Mistress of Liberty shook her fist, with its torch, screening with her rear end the prison on the Island of Tears.

We are on the open, return-voyage ocean. For a day there has been neither rolling nor drinking. American territorial waters still flow under the dry law of abstinence. Within another day, we were to have both. People lay flat out.

Remaining on deck and in the dining rooms, there were about twenty people, including the officers.

Six of these were the young Americans: a novelist, two artists, a poet, a musician and a young girl seeing him off, who had clambered on board and who, in the cause of love, had sailed away even without a French visa.

These representatives of art, taking cognisance of the lack both of parents and prohibition, began drinking.

At about five they started on cocktails; over dinner they downed all the table wine; after dinner they ordered champagne. In the ten minutes before the bar closed they pried up bottles between every finger. After drinking all those, they mooched around the swaying corridors in pursuit of the slumbering waiter.

They finished drinking the day before we sailed in – in the first place, because the steward, infuriated by the continual racket, promised on oath to hand the two artists over to the

French police before their feet could touch the shore. Secondly, the entire stocks of champagne had now been drunk. This may also serve to explain the steward's severity.

This coterie apart, a bald old Canadian hung around pestering me with his love for Russians, solicitously naming, and enquiring about my associations with all the former princes, living and dead, who had ever graced the pages of the newspapers.

Two diplomats shambled around between the clattering tables: the assistant to the Paraguayan Consul in London and the Chilean representative to the League of Nations. The Paraguayan drank willingly enough, but never placed an order himself, and always in the manner of studying etiquette and keeping his eye on the young Americans. The Chilean took advantage of every minute of brighter weather, and any sortie by women up on deck, in order to put his temperament on display, or at least get himself photographed with someone against the background of a siren or a funnel. And finally there was a Spanish businessman who didn't know a word of English, and in French could only say '*regardez*!'. He didn't seem even to know *merci*. But the Spaniard acquitted himself so skilfully with this word that, with gestures and smiles added, for days on end he scuttled from group to group in a positive conversational frenzy.

Again and again the newspaper came out, they laid wagers on the rate of knots, or they celebrated a tombola win.

In the solitude of the return voyage, I tried to formulate my essential American impressions.

FIRST. The futurism of naked technology, of a surface impressionism of smoke and cables, which has the enormous task of revolutionising the congealed, swollen backwoods psyche – this primitive futurism is definitively confirmed by America.

Invitation and pontification are not needed here. Bring Fordsons to Novorossisk, in the same way that Amtorg does.[60]

LEF's mission looms in front of the workers of art: not to eulogise technology, but to harness it in the name of humanity's interests.[61] Not aesthetic slobbering over iron fire escapes on skyscrapers, but the straightforward organisation of living space.

And what about the automobile? There are vast numbers of automobiles, and it's time to think of ways to stop them from stinking out the streets.

No skyscrapers – in which you can't live, though people do.

The overhead trains spit dust from under their wheels as they go scudding past, and the trains seem to be running over your ears.

It's not a question of eulogising the din, but fitting silencers – we poets need to converse on the trains.

Motorless flight, wireless telegraph, radio, buses that will displace trams on rails, subway systems that will take under ground all that is visible.

It may be that tomorrow's technology, increasing human powers a million-fold, will go down the route of eradicating building sites, din and other such trappings of today's technology.

SECOND. The division of labour is destructive of human means of livelihood. The capitalist, having separated out and allocated a percentage of workers of material value to himself (certain specialists, tame union bosses, etc.), treats the remaining working masses like inexhaustible goods.

If we want to, we sell; if we want to, we buy. If you don't agree to work, we sit it out; if you go on strike, we take on others. We look after the subordinate and the capable; and for the insubordinate, it's the batons of the official police, and the Mausers and the Colts of the private dicks.

The cunning splitting of the working class – into the run-of-the-mill and the privileged; the ignorance of workers sucked dry by labour, who, after a thoroughly systematised working day, are not even left with sufficient energy needed to be able to think; the comparative prosperity of the worker able to hammer out a subsistence wage; the delusory hope of riches in the future, given added relish by insistent anecdotes of billionaires who started off as cleaners; the absolute military fortresses on many a street corner, and the menacing word 'deportation' – these push into the distance any significant hopes there may be of revolutionary outbursts in America. Only perhaps if a revolutionary Europe refused payment of some of its debts. Or if, on a paw stretched over the Pacific Ocean, the Japanese should start trimming their talons. Therefore, the assimilation of American technology and efforts towards a second discovery of America – for the benefit of the U.S.S.R. – is a job for everyone travelling through the Americas.

THIRD. It's possible, this fantasy. America is growing fatter. People worth a mere two million dollars are considered modest upstarts.

Everyone is loaned money – even the Pope of Rome who bought a palace opposite, in order that the inquisitive shouldn't be looking in at his papal windows.

This money is taken from all over the place – even from the unfilled purse of the American workers.

The banks engage in a frenzied campaign to get hold of workers' savings.

These deposits gradually create the belief that you need to be concerned with the percentages, not with the work.

America will become just a financial centre, a money-broker of a country.

The ex-workers, who have yet to pay off the instalments on their car, and on a microscopic house so flooded in sweat that it's no surprise if it's even got upstairs: to these former workers it can seem as though the main thing is to check that their papal money hasn't just vanished.

It could happen that the United States will jointly turn out to be the final armed defenders of a hopeless bourgeois cause – then history will be able to write a good Wellsian novel of *The War of the Worlds*.[62]

The aim of my sketches is to induce study of America's weaknesses and strengths, in anticipation of the prolonged struggle ahead.

The *Rochambeau* approached Le Havre. Ignorant little buildings, whose storeys need counting only on your fingers: the harbour is an hour away; and already when we were tying up, the quayside was dotted with ragged cripples and urchins.

Unwanted coppers were thrown from the decks (it is considered 'lucky'), and the urchins, crushing one another, wrenching at tattered shirts with teeth and fingers, got really stuck in to these coins.

The Americans laughed unctuously from the deck and took instant snapshots.

These beggars loom before me as a symbol of the Europe to come – if there is no cessation to the grovelling before American – and anyone else's – money.

We were travelling towards Paris, punching through, by means of tunnels, the endless hills that lay across our route.

By comparison with America, you see pitiful shacks here. Every inch of land has been seized through age-old struggle, has been exhausted through the ages, and with pharmaceutical prejudice has been exploited for violets or lettuce. But even this contemptible attachment to the cottage, to the strip of land, to what is one's own, even this deliberate age-old clinging, now struck me as a prodigious culture in comparison to the bivouac structure, the self-seeking character, of American life.

On the other hand, all the way to Rouen, along the endless chestnut-lined country roads, going through the densest patch in France, we met only one automobile.

– 1925–1926

How I Made Her Laugh

Probably foreigners have some respect for me, but it's also possible they consider me an idiot – I won't say anything about Russians for the moment. You've only got to take my American situation: they've invited over a poet – so they've been told, a genius. Genius – that's even better than famous. So I turn up, and straight away I say:

'Gif mi pliz sem tee!'

OK. They give me some. I wait a while – and once more:

'Gif mi pliz…'

Again they give me some.

And I do it again and again, in different tones of voice and varying my expression:

'Gif mi yeh sem tee, sem tee yeh gif mi,' I enunciate. And so the evening rolls on.

Alert, deferential old men listen, admire and think: 'Oh, that's the Russian for you, won't say a word more than he has to. A thinker… Tolstoy… The North.'

An American only thinks at work. It won't enter an American's head to think after six o'clock.

It won't enter his head that I don't have a word of English, that my tongue is jumping up and down and twisting like a corkscrew from the urge to speak, that, hoisting my tongue like a hoopla ring, I am desperately trying to string together in a comprehensible manner the various requisite vowels and consonants. It wouldn't enter an American's head that I am convulsively giving birth to wild supra-English phrases:

'Yess, oowite pliz fife dobble arm strong…'

And it seems to me that, enchanted by my pronunciation, captivated by my wit, won over by the profundity of my thought, girls with legs a metre long are left stupefied, while men shrink in the eyes of everyone as they become totally depressed at the utter impossibility of ever outperforming me.

But the ladies back away, on hearing for the hundredth time the plea for tea uttered in my pleasant low bass voice, and the gentlemen disperse to the corners, reverentially mouthing wise-cracks at my tongue-tied expense.

'Translate this for them,' I yell to Burliuk,[63] 'tell them that, if only they knew Russian, I could, without as much as a blemish on their dicky shirt, nail them with my tongue to the crosses of their own braces, I could twirl the whole verminous collection of them round the skewer of my tongue...'

And the well-meaning Burliuk translates for me:

'My great friend Vladimir Vladimirovich would like another cup of tea.'

All right, then.

I'll make my excuses at home.

I'll have something to say!

I'll say something that will send the humourless editor of *Crocodile* into paroxysms. I'll say something that will cause stern court officials who list furniture for confiscation for the non-payment of tax – a widow's furniture, a hungry old woman's – these sternest of bureaucrats, at the risk of losing their jobs, to explode with laughter at the merest recollection of my words.

And so here I am, at home.

You will understand me.

With mouth wide open, with a word already a-droop from my lips, I rush off everywhere where there's even the slightest hope of speaking.

At the risk of arousing fantastic suspicions, I involve myself in the sad conversations of frontier guards delving through people's trunks. I butt into the domestic quarrel of some Red Army man and his woman and, having momentarily shut them up, I put the whole family to flight. In a state of high oratorical tension, I stand blocking the corridor of a railway carriage, ready to assail the first emerging person with stale questions and answers.

For the orator, the cross-border train is a bad investment. The compartment to the right is full of Japanese, and their language is Japanese; to the left there's a silent Frenchman, opening his startled eyes ever wider with each fresh kilometre of Russian snow.

Just one compartment struck me as even remotely open to any question of possible russified chat, and so I laid a well-planned siege.

An hour ago a man in a scarf sneaked through, cheerfully bellowing, to no one in particular:

'They've given fifteen degrees of frost, and I can't see ten!'

Who gives them to him? Why fifteen? Why can't he see them? I don't understand a word of this.

He bellowed it out, slammed the door and chained it.

After another hour the snoring from behind the door persuaded me to relax my siege. I catnapped somehow and at seven in the morning was already taking up my post.

At eleven a door flew open and a woman appeared, giving off a whiff of everything foreign.

She held in her hand a huge toothbrush – although gold, I should think, would be better cleaned with chamois leather.[64]

The woman purposefully addressed herself to me:

'Who is in the bathroom?'

I had no prepared answer for this and just sort of shrugged it off.

'Didn't you notice?' said the woman, and with such contempt that I just cringed back into my seat all the way to Moscow. I had given up on speaking. I had no arguments. I had travelled all the way from New York, I somehow didn't notice Moscow, and had nearly got all the way to Krasnodar. All the same, I am going to be speaking.

I'm going to be speaking to Cossack men and women. Krasnodar – that's the capital of Adygea,[65] not a corridor; not some miserable corridor, mark you, owned by an international sleeping-car company.

Words and phrases had already accumulated over the day, and I had already chewed them over in such a way that any speakers of the infinite Russian language could not help but – indeed they absolutely must – laugh.

On the first person I meet, I told myself, dragging my suitcase up to the second floor of the First Soviet hotel, on the very first person, I'll try out the hilarious power of words.

At eight o'clock in the morning hotels are still empty, but I pressed the full complement of bells indicated by the white notice stuck on the wall.

In came a young, attractive, large woman.

'I want some tea,' I said, quite properly reckoning to draw her into conversation by resorting to crockery talk.

The thing was to gain her confidence. Helping her lift the samovar, I cheerfully asked:

'Do you talk to people in Russian, or in Adyghe?'[66]

'What?' she threw back at me.

'Well, I've just come from the Ukraine, and there's a signpost I saw there: on the right it's written "*Bakhmach*" for Russians, and on the left the same – "*Bakhmach*", only for Ukrainians.'

'That's so they don't get confused,' she concurred sympathetically.

'And in your town is there an Engels Street and a Lunacharsky Lane?'

'Which ones are they?' she asked.

Noting the lack of corresponding spirit in her replies, I moved on to more everyday topics.

'They wouldn't serve me shashlik last night in the *dukhan*.[67] A bad year for lambs.'

'There weren't many lambs, it's true,' she agreed, having now finished her crockery arrangements, and evidently struggling to get any purchase on the direction of my conversation.

'In my sleeping compartment,' I went on, raising my voice and losing my self-control, 'they put this man in with me, a little guy and a real deadbeat, it took him half an hour to get dressed in the morning. I said to him, "Why are you so lethargic? I have a hard enough time getting dressed, but you – you're only in short trousers!"'

The woman flushed, frowned and snapped back:

'That's quite enough about trousers and getting them off. I'm a trade-union member!' she said and left the room, slamming the door.

Feeling embittered and insulted, I spread out my portable rubber bathtub, stamped off to the W.C. and, without going in search of the chambermaid, yelled out into thin air:

'A bucket of cold water for room 16!'

Coming back from the W.C., I suddenly started. I stood stock-still. A sound of laughter reached me. This laughter reaching me came from my room. On the tips of my toes I moved stealthily, like a sleepwalker, over to my goal, to the chink. I want to see this, I want to shake the hand of whoever has managed to make this monumental woman laugh.

Consumed with envy, I poked my face into the crevice in the door. The woman was standing over my rubber bath, the woman was leaning against the rubber bath, her eyes streaming with tears of mirth, and shrieking with laughter. She was laughing so much that waves were billowing across the bathwater, in an ebbing and flowing quite uncharacteristic of stagnant water that unified the rubber bath with the sea.

That day I had learnt a great deal: regarding both the difficulty of the writer's craft, and the relativity of humour.

– 1926

Three Poems about America

The Atlantic Ocean

The stone of Spain
                    is blinding and white,
and its walls –
               like the teeth of saws.
The boat
          until twelve
                   was eating coal
and of fresh water drinking its fill.
Shuffling,
          the boat,
                  its fettered snout
and at one,
snuffling,
          it sucked in its anchor
                     and made off.
Europe
          stole away, growing small.
Running
          alongside
                  are aquatic bulges,
as immense
          as the years.
Above me the birds,
                below me the fish,
and around –
          the water.
For weeks
          through its athletic chest –
now workaholic,
               now crazy alcoholic –
the Atlantic

Ocean
               sighs and thunders
its best.
'My idea, fellers,
is to sneak up to the Sahara...
then open up and spit –
below there's a boat.
I can sink it,
I can keep it afloat.
Let's have you dry –
for fish soup.
Passengers are no good to us –
they don't make much of a dinner.
I won't bother with it...
                    okay...
let them sail on...'
Waves
        are masters
                  of agitation:
they can splash up your childhood;
                        or else –
                        your lover's voice.
For me,
        there again,
                they can put out the flags!
There –
        it's off again,
                rumbling,
                        smashing about!
Then once more
        the clear water's
                calmed down,
and there are

no concerns over anyone.
When suddenly,
                from somewhere –
                            hell knows where! –
comes up
        from the depths
                        an aqueous Revolutionary Committee.
And an army of drops –
                    aquatic partisans –
scrabble
        up
            from their oceanic pits,
flinging themselves sky high
                        and dropping back anew,
their porphyry foam ripped to shreds.
Yet again
        the waters have pooled into one,
commanding
            the wave
                    to seethe like a war chief.
Then the surf sinks
                from under a cloud
                            right to the bottom –
decrees
        and slogans
                pour forth like rain.
And waves
            swear
                to the all-aquatic committee
not to lay down
            their weapons of storm
                            'til victory come.
And now they've won –

to the equator runs the circle
of the Soviet-drops' boundless sway.
Minor meetings of backward waves
kick up
about something
in pompous tones.
So now
the ocean,
smiling neat and clean,
has stilled
for a while
to a peaceful tone.
I watch from the rail.
Do your utmost, my friends!
Under the ladder,
hanging there
like a fragile bridge,
dealing with its oceanic agenda
sweats away
over something
a local waves' council.
And underwater
efficiently on the quiet
into a palace
grows
a wickerwork of corals,
to ease the life
of the working she-whale
with her bread-winning whale
and pre-school whale-babe.
Already
the moon too
they've laid as a path.

Straight off,
            on your belly,
                        crawl on, it's dry!
Enemies won't butt in –
                        skyward
                                    guardingly
there watches,
            unblinkingly,
                        the Atlantic eye.
Now you chill
            in the gleam of the moon's lacquer,
now you moan,
            doused in a lather of wounds.
I look,
        and look –
                    and ever the same,
the ocean to me stays near and dear.
Evermore
            your crashing
                        will be in my ear.
In my eyes
            gladly
                    you will be spilling.
In your breadth,
            in your action,
                        in blood,
                                    and in spirit –
of my revolution
            you're the elder sibling.

Brooklyn Bridge

Let's hear it, Coolidge,[68]
your joyful cry!
For what's good
                    I too won't stint on the words.
From these praises,
                blush redder
                            than the flag of our own soil,
though indeed you be
                  the all-united states
                          of
America.
Just as to his church
                creeps
                    the deranged believer,
as though
           retreating to a cloister,
                      strict and frugal –
so I
    in an evening
                greying semblance
walk,
        in all humility, onto Brooklyn Bridge.
Just as into
              a subjugated city
                      the conqueror shoves
his cannons – their muzzles
                  giraffe-high –
so I, inebriated in eulogy,
                ready to feast,
mount,
        feeling proud,

                        onto Brooklyn Bridge.
As a fatuous artist
                        on a museum's madonna
thirsts his eye,
                        lovesick and keen,
so I,
        down from the heavens,
                                scattered to the stars,
look
        upon New York
                        through Brooklyn Bridge.
New York,
                until evening so tough
                                and sultry,
has forgotten
                its toughness,
                                and its height,
and only
            house-sprites' souls
appear
            in the translucence of fenestral light.
Here
        there's scarcely a tingle
                                of an elevated chuff.
And only
            by such
                    quiet tingling
can you know –
                    trains
                            run jangling through,
with sounds
            like clearing dishes in the buffet.
And when,

or thus it seemed, from where a rivulet starts
a tradesman
                    is delivering
                              sugar from his mill –
it's just
          passing-through masts below bridge,
of a size
          no more than pin-sized.
I'm proud
          of this very mile of steel,
that's where alive
                    my visions can arise –
a struggle
          for constructions
                              over style,
severe reckonings
                    of screws
                              and steel.
If there
          should come
                    an end to the world –
and chaos
          would rip
                    the planet asunder,
and just
          the one remaining thing
                              should be this,
above the dust of ruin this rearing bridge,
then,
          just as from bones even leaner than needles,
they fatten up
                    big lizards
                              that stand in museums,

so
   from this bridge
                   a geologist of the epochs
would succeed
             in recreating
                      the days of now.
He will say:
             'So this is
                 the paw of steel
that united
         the seas with the prairies,
and it's from here
              Europe
                  strained to the West,
having scattered
          Indian feathers
                   to the winds.
There's memory
         of machinery
                in this rib –
just imagine,
           would hands suffice,
placing
       a steel foot
             on Manhattan,
to haul up
        Brooklyn
            by the lip?
By the leads
        of electrical strands –
I know –
      it's the era
            following steam –

it's when
        people
                already
                        yelled over radio,
it's when
        people
                already
                        flew by plane.
It's when
        living
                was
                        for some – free and easy,
for others –
        a hungry
                and extended howl.
It's from here
        that the jobless
into the Hudson
        pitched
                head first.
And beyond this
        my picture
                becomes snag-free,
and on cable-like strings
                it plays right up to the stars.
I can see –
        that here
                stood Mayakovsky:
here he stood,
        synthesising his strophes by the syllable.'
I keep looking at it,
        like an Eskimo at a train,
sticking at it,

      like ticks stick to ears.
Brooklyn Bridge –
yeah...
      It's something else!

Homeward!

Get going, thoughts, off home with you!
Embrace,
            depths of soul and sea!
Anyone
        who's permanently lucid
is,
   in my view,
             unremittingly stupid.
I'm in the worst cabin
               of all cabins –
all night, above my head,
                feet hammer away.
All night,
        wrecking the ceiling's peace,
the dance drags on,
             with the wailing refrain:
'Marquita,
        Marquita,
Marquita my love,
Oh why,
        Oh Marquita,
Can't you love me true…'
And why
        would Marquita love me?!
I haven't
        as much as a franc to burn.
But Marquita
        (make-a-wink-at-her!) –
and for a hundred francs
             she'll do you a turn.
For modest sums now –

you can be quite chic –
but no,
        clever clogs,
                    fluffing up your greasy locks,
you'd palm her off
                    with a sewing machine,
that'll stitch
            in silk
                    your seamed-up eclogues.
Proletarians
            get to Communism
                            bent low –
by the low road of mines,
                        pitchfork,
                                and sickle –
while I,
        from poetic heights,
                        dive into the Communist flow,
for without it,
            for me,
                    love is too fickle.
It's all the same –
                I banish myself,
                                or get sent packing –
my verbal steel rusts,
                    my brass bass will blacken.
Why
    under foreign downpours
should I soak,
                rot through
                            and corrode?
Here I lie,
        while traversing the water,

too lazy
        to even start
                my bodily motor.
I feel myself
        to be a Soviet
                factory,
turning out happiness.
I don't want,
        like a flower from the glades,
to be plucked,
        official weight pulled.
I want
        State Planning
                to sweat in debates,
over my
        assignments for the year.
I want
        the commissar of these times
hanging over my thoughts with his command.
I want
        my heart to be apportioned
heaps of love
        in a super ration.
I want
        the factory committee
                when work is done
to secure my lips
        by lock.
I want
        the bayonet
                equated with the pen.
And that, along with pig-iron,
                and figures of steel in,

verse output

        should concern the Politburo,

and reports

        be delivered by Stalin.

'And so on, they say,

         and so forth...

           And the very peaks

we've scaled

        from our workers' lairs:

in the Union

        of Republics

          comprehension of verse

has exceeded

        our pre-war norms...'

I want to be understood by my land,

But if I'm not understood –

          well, fine!

Through my native land

         I'll pass sideways on,

just as

      the slanting rain slides by.

Notes

1. Acronym of Moscow's famous 'State Department Store'.

2. N.F. Baliev: manager and impresario of the Moscow cabaret 'The Bat', who in the 1920s emigrated and toured America; F.I. Shaliapin [Chaliapin] (1873–1938): famous Russian bass singer, who never returned to Russia from a 1921 foreign tour.

3. An affectation of Jewish-Russian pronunciation.

4. This was the period of prohibition in much of the U.S.A.

5. A cigar manufacturer, also mentioned in Mayakovsky's poem 'Black and White' (*Blek end uait*, 1925).

6. Kuznetsky Most: a fashionable Moscow thoroughfare; Prado: Havana's main street; Vedado: a rich suburb of Havana.

7. In a note to his poem, 'Black and White', Mayakovsky explains that *colario* is a flower from Havana.

8. Hotel porters used to wear numbered armbands identifying them as authorised workers.

9. James Fenimore Cooper (1789–1851), American author of pioneer life, and Mayne Reid (1818–83), American writer of adventure novels.

10. Central American turkey buzzards.

11. Diego Rivera (1886–1957) was a Mexican artist famous for his murals, influenced by Native American art.

12. The (Mexican) eponymous hero of a novel (of 1922) by Il'ia Erenburg (1891–1967), in which Rivera makes an appearance.

13. President of Mexico, 1924–28.

14. Perhaps Mayakovsky is confusing this with a 'Nemean lion': the beast killed by Hercules as his first labour.

15. 'Social commission' (or 'demand': *sotsial'nyi zakaz*) was a slogan propagated by Mayakovsky's LEF (Left Front of Arts) faction in Soviet culture, advocating the pre-eminence of social content, and was later co-opted into 'socialist realism'.

16. Aleksandr Blok's narrative poem *The Twelve* (*Dvenadtsat'*) and Mayakovsky's short agitational poem 'Left March' (*Levyi marsh*) were two prominent (and very distinct) revolutionary works produced in 1918.

17. Anna Pavlova (1882–1931), Russian-born ballet dancer, famous for her world tours.

18. A low-class variety establishment, presumably named after the Parisian variety theatre, originally the Grand Café Chinois and Théâtre BA-TA-CLAN, founded in 1865 (French).

19. President of Mexico 1877–80 and 1884–1911.

20. Agustín de Iturbide (1783–1824) was self-declared emperor of Mexico, 1822–23.

21. Thomas Cook & Son (now Thomas Cook, Ltd), travel agents.

22. These lines reflect Mayakovsky's childhood reading of the works of James Fenimore Cooper and Mayne Reid (see note 9), who were popular among the young in Russia at the time.

23. Samuel Gompers (1850–1924), a British-born American union leader.

24. General secretary to the Soviet plenipotentiary in Mexico at that time.

25. Mayakovsky's 'folk etymology' of *gringo* may here be questionable (apart from the song running 'green *grow* the rushes, oh'). Dictionaries (e.g. Webster) link the word to *griego*: 'Greek', or 'foreigner'.

26. These and the following lines are taken (almost exactly) from the end of Mayakovsky's poem 'Mexico', dated 20th July 1925.

27. A reference to fortune-telling organ-grinders being accompanied by monkeys and parrots that picked a fortune slip.

28. Mayakovsky is here said to be mistaking Pennsylvania Station with Grand Central Station (and its star-studded ceiling).

29. 10th September 1925.

30. The Industrial Workers of the World, an international union founded in the U.S.A. in 1905, dedicated to the overthrow of state power; its influence was in decline by the 1920s. Morris Hillquit had earlier led his wing of Socialist Labor into the moderate Socialist Party of America.

31. General Richard Mulcahy had commanded the Irish Free State army in the civil war, thus incurring the wrath of Irish republicans.

32. Calvin Coolidge was thirtieth president of the U.S.A., from 1923 to 1929.

33. Sergei Rachmaninov (1873–1943) had emigrated from Russia at the onset of the Revolution and settled mainly in the United States, where he acquired an immense reputation as a concert pianist.

34. The reference is to Ganna Walska (second wife of one Harold Fowler McCormick), a Polish operatic singer of less than the highest musical reputation.

35. 'Russian mountains': here an extended stretch of roller-coaster, or scenic railway.

36. Mayakovsky may here be applying the nickname of a certain wealthy financier (James Buchanan Brady, 1856–1917) to the subject of an unconnected anecdote of reckless spending.

37. The prosecution brought (July 1925) against the teaching of the theory of evolution in Dayton, Tennessee.

38. Sic.

39. The alternative view on offer is that Sigman, president of the I.L.G.W.U. (International Ladies' Garment Workers Union) from 1923 to 1928, prevented a Communist takeover of the union.

40. A Yiddish daily Communist newspaper, published from 1922.

41. Shapurji Saklatvala (1874–1936), an Indian-born member of the U.K. parliament, whose visa, granted for attendance at a Washington conference

in 1923, was revoked by the U.S. government. Saklatvala was the Communist Party MP for North Battersea (elected with Labour Party support) from 1922 to 1923 and 1924 to 1929.

42. V.G. Korolenko (1853–1921) visited America in 1893.

43. Maxim Gorky (1868–1936) visited America in 1906, writing an 'offensive' pamphlet entitled 'The City of the Yellow Devil' (*Gorod zheltogo d'iavola*).

44. A notorious criminal case of 1924, in which two teenagers admitted killing a younger boy, to learn 'what a murderer thinks'.

45. This was the infamous case of Sacco and Vanzetti, which took on a particular political notoriety; the two were eventually executed by the state of Massachusetts in 1927.

46. The works of O. Henry, pseudonym of William Sydney Porter (1862–1910), and the Nick Carter detective novels – written by various authors – were widely read in Soviet Russia; Lev Kuleshov (1899–1970) was a prominent Soviet film director; cowboy (or check) shirts were popular there in the 1920s (especially in cinematic circles).

47. One particularly harshly treated case of this crime in Russia gave rise to the expression: 'They'll burn you like the horse-thieves in Listviany'.

48. *Opportunity: A Journal of Negro Life* was published by the interracial National Urban League from 1923 to 1949.

49. Alexander Pushkin and Alexandre Dumas (*père*) had a black great-grand-parent and grandparent respectively; 'Henry Tan': Mayakovsky is presumed to be referring to the black painter Henry Ossawa Tanner (1859–1937).

50. Mayakovsky's lengthy epic poem *150,000,000* was written in 1919 and published in 1920; the title refers to the then population of the U.S.S.R. and the poem depicts an epic struggle between capitalist U.S.A. and the proletarian simplicity of Soviet Russia.

51. Mayakovsky plays here with the Russian word *chudno*. Stressed on the second syllable, it means 'strange'; with the stress on the first, it means 'marvellous'. Mayakovsky here omits the words 'and wonderful' (*chúdno*), following the final words quoted in the poem's original.

52. Carl Sandburg (1878–1967), a major poet of the mid-West and of urban populist feelings, and the collector of folk-ballads. Mayakovsky and Sandburg met briefly at the *Chicago Tribune*, conversing through an interpreter.

53. Four of these defendants were hanged and one (Lingg) committed suicide in 1887, following a trial arising from the violent events in Chicago of May 1886. In 1893 the governor of Illinois declared the trial to have been a farce, pardoning three surviving prisoners. A monument to those executed was erected in the same year.

54. Presumably, in this 'count', Mayakovsky is excluding New York.

55. Followers of General Wrangel (1878–1928), the most prominent military leader of the defeated Whites in the Russian Civil War.

56. The wife of Kiril Romanov, a pretender to the Russian throne after the execution of Tsar Nicholas II.

57. Brother of Kiril Romanov.

58. Aleksandr Rodchenko (1891–1956), a prominent Soviet avant-garde artist, specialist in photomontage, and a friend of Mayakovsky's.

59. Henry Ford's *My Life and Work* (1922), when published in Russian translation (G. Ford, *Moia rabota i zhizn'*, Petrograd, 1923) became recommended reading among the captains of Soviet industry.

60. Fordson: Ford-made tractors, imported into the U.S.S.R. in the 1920s; Amtorg, a U.S.-Soviet trading corporation, founded in 1924, at whose New York headquarters on Fifth Avenue Mayakovsky stayed.

61. See note 15 above.

62. The science fiction of H.G. Wells was popular in Russia. Wells published *The War of the Worlds*, dealing with a Martian invasion of Earth, in serial form in 1897.

63. David Burliuk (1882–1967), Russian Futurist poet and painter, and a former guru to the young Mayakovsky, who had been living in the U.S.A. from 1922.

64. Gold teeth are very common in Russia.

65. A region in the North Caucasus, since 1993 a Republic within the Russian Federation (the present capital is Maykop).

66. The local (Caucasian) language of Adygea, perhaps better known as Circassian.

67. A Caucasian inn.

68. Calvin Coolidge (See note 32 above).

Biographical note

Vladimir Vladimirovich Mayakovsky was born into a family of 'non-landed gentry' on 19th July 1893 in Baghdadi, Kutais region (temporarily renamed, through much of the Soviet era, 'Mayakovsky'), in Georgia – then part of the Russian Empire. He attended the gymnasium at Kutais; a school in Moscow; the Stroganov School of Industrial Arts; and finally, from 1911 to 1914, the Moscow Institute of Painting, Sculpture and Architecture. A member of the Moscow committee of the Bolshevik faction of the Russian Social Democratic Party from as early as 1908, he was arrested for political agitation and imprisoned for six months in 1909. Associated with Futurist circles from 1912 (especially 'Hylaea', the Cubo-Futurist grouping), he participated in the iconoclastic manifesto *A Slap in the Face of Public Taste* in 1912, and was subsequently the editor of a number of avant-garde artistic and politico-literary publications. He produced an innovative play, *Vladimir Mayakovsky: A Tragedy*, in 1913 and his poetry, scattered in Futurist publications from 1912, began to appear in earnest from 1915. He was drafted into the Petrograd Military Automobile School, serving from 1915 to 1917. He also became well known for his appearances at the Poets' Café in Moscow. A strong supporter of the October Revolution, Mayakovsky took a leading role as a writer and propagandist in support of the new Bolshevik state. An artist and silent film actor, as well as the leading avant-garde poet, he designed posters and wrote short plays and other texts for the Russian Telegraph Agency (ROSTA) from 1919 to 1921. During much of the 1920s he travelled widely in Europe and America. He was the co-founder, with Osip Brik, of *LEF* ('Left Front of Art'), and then *Novyi LEF* ('New Left Front'). In addition to a rich body of narrative poems and lyric verse, he wrote two prominent satirical plays, *The Bedbug* and *The Bathhouse* (produced 1929 and 1930). On 14th April 1930, apparently for a mixture of personal and political reasons, Mayakovsky committed suicide (an action prefigured in a number of his works).

Neil Cornwell is the author of a number of books (including *The Literary Fantastic*, *James Joyce and the Russians*, and *Vladimir Nabokov*). He is the editor of the *Reference Guide to Russian Literature* and *The Routledge Companion to Russian Literature* and has translated volumes of the selected writings of Vladimir Odoevsky (*The Salamander and other Gothic Tales*) and Daniil Kharms (*Incidences*). He is Professor of Russian and Comparative Literature at the University of Bristol.

HESPERUS PRESS

Hesperus Press, as suggested by the Latin motto, is committed to bringing near what is far – far both in space and time. Works written by the greatest authors, and unjustly neglected or simply little known in the English-speaking world, are made accessible through new translations and a completely fresh editorial approach. Through these classic works, the reader is introduced to the greatest writers from all times and all cultures.

For more information on Hesperus Press, please visit our website: **www.hesperuspress.com**

ET REMOTISSIMA PROPE

MODERN VOICES

SELECTED TITLES FROM HESPERUS PRESS

Author	Title	Foreword writer
Mikhail Bulgakov	*A Dog's Heart*	A.S. Byatt
Mikhail Bulgakov	*The Fatal Eggs*	Doris Lessing
F. Scott Fitzgerald	*The Popular Girl*	Helen Dunmore
F. Scott Fitzgerald	*The Rich Boy*	John Updike
Franz Kafka	*Metamorphosis*	Martin Jarvis
Franz Kafka	*The Trial*	Zadie Smith
Carlo Levi	*Words are Stones*	Anita Desai
André Malraux	*The Way of the Kings*	Rachel Seiffert
Katherine Mansfield	*In a German Pension*	Linda Grant
Katherine Mansfield	*Prelude*	William Boyd
Luigi Pirandello	*Loveless Love*	
Jean-Paul Sartre	*The Wall*	Justin Cartwright